WOLVES AND INSURANCE

Mentally Preparing for the Insurance Business

JOHN BROWN JR.

PAGE PUBLISHING, INC.
New York, NY

First originally published by Page Publishing, Inc. 2017

ISBN 978-1-64027-439-6 (Paperback)
ISBN 978-1-64027-440-2 (Digital)

Printed in the United States of America

To my loving wife Alisia and beautiful daughter Amaya.
I love you more than words can describe.....

INTRODUCTION

Insurance has always been widely regarded as one of the most lucrative and rewarding businesses in the corporate world. I would have to agree wholeheartedly because I have been in the business for over a decade now. There is definitely something to be said about a business that is focused on protecting the assets of families, businesses, entities, etc. It is the primary job of an insurance agent to deeply consider what their clients have worked so hard for their entire lives and to make sure they secure those interests with care and extreme attention to detail.

It has always been a lifetime dream of mine to write a book that was geared to help others with what I struggled with early in my insurance career. Most of what I struggled with was understanding why there were preconceived and unfavorable notions that the general public had about insurance and insurance agents alike. I was not prepared and was truly blindsided and confused by this. Now, we have all read books that were specifically written to help aspiring insurance agents grow their perspective business. I, myself, have read them all. There are guides out there to help you network, ask for referrals, advertise, etc. The list goes on and on. All these books and manuscripts are extremely helpful in helping the aspiring agent grow an insurance business. I absolutely suggest reading as many of them as you can. Getting different ideas from other success stories can really help you cultivate your own business plan, ideology, and goals. As insurance agents, we all know that referrals are the nucleus of how our business will continuously grow. If there is one book on getting referrals, there are a million. Read them all.

Wolves and Insurance is different. To most, the title may suggest a look into a cutthroat business in which only the strong survives. Or like in most sales businesses, you have to be a wolf in order to get what you want out of your clients. Perhaps you are also thinking that it suggests implementing a wolf-sheep approach. You know that approach, don't you? It's where the wolf dresses in sheep's clothing and coexists in the sheep population, only to surface and strike at any moment of vulnerability. Well, you are wrong. This isn't Wall Street.

We all know the fundamentals to growing an insurance business. We, as professionals, have all attended trainings and seminars that are designed to help us put an action plan together and carry out specific duties that have had proven successful to most. There is always the mentor approach as well. I'm sure you know this one as well. This is where you reach out to successful agents within your industry in hopes to get different ideas and practices that make them successful. Mentors have always been a comfortable approach to most because, for the most part, successful agents have no problem sharing their ideas and practices. Well, this book is not about sales processes or designing business plans. In all my years of insurance, I have learned that having a solid business plan and goals is only half the battle. The other side of the coin is more psychological.

I am fairly sure that you have spent hours upon hours thinking about what you need to do to become a better insurance agent. This causes us to branch out and explore the ideas that I have already mentioned above, i.e., books, seminars, mentors. In doing this, I have always believed that this approach does help, but only hands you a set of specific instructions and processes to "get sales." It's what you do once you obtain those instructions that matters. Different ideas about goal setting and networking are effective only if you choose to put in the work and devise a specific plan to move forward with your newly discovered ideas. That is the easy part.

Upon reading this book, I will ask you to not forget all that you have learned about being an insurance professional up to this point. One of the most rewarding aspects of being an insurance agent is cultivating your business using these ideas that you have collected over the years. It does not matter if you are new to the business or tenured.

I was once new to the business as well as thousands of others. What we will discuss in this book will help you no matter how experienced. Perhaps for those that are new to this business, it may benefit you more to be mentally prepared before implementing action.

In the insurance business, you deal with several different entities daily. Not only do you have to be well versed with the portfolio of products you offer, but you also have to deal with claims service, underwriters, administrative staff, etc. Having multiple irons in the fire doesn't quite describe it. It is for this reason that I believe that mental conditioning is of the upmost importance in this business. There is never a bad time to positively cultivate your mentality. Deciding what kind of agent you want to be will only help your cause in the future.

In *Wolves and Insurance*, I will help you identify the preconceived notions you will run into during your insurance career that have been the consensus for many years. Not only will we identify them, but we will also learn to adapt to them and overcome them when they are negative in nature. Remember, you deal with the public. These scenarios will include your clients, your competition, and most importantly, you. Yes, I really said *you*. You have to understand that an effective insurance agent learns to adapt to the environment at hand. No two people are the same. This holds true with your competition as well. You have to be able to not only identify this but also overcome it by providing solutions to help mend broken fences that exists by no fault of your own. This all comes back to *you*.

I firmly believe that the success you will have in the insurance business depends on how frequently you put your clients' interests ahead of your own. Alas, it does come back to you! I am a realist, and I do understand that there are many things that can happen in life that can cause a change in thought and action. As so in the insurance business. You may deal with an irate client that can absolutely impact you negatively. Or on the other side of the coin, you can have immense success and let monetary advances change who you are as an agent and how you take care of your clients. The point that I am trying to make is that I believe that if you keep your core as an agent, the consistency that will manifest itself will ultimately build trust in those you encounter daily in your business. In other words, do not let the situation change who you are as an agent. Adaptation will be the key.

Wolves and Insurance will put into perspective the good and bad elements in the insurance business on a more emotionally driven arena. By analyzing those around you, you can slowly begin to discover who you are as a business person and provide light to your clients when they are otherwise conditioned to the opposite. We will learn to use observation with our clients to better serve them and, thus, grow our business. Yes, by conforming to your surroundings mentally, you can grow your business. How, you ask? By better understanding your clients, you will know what approach you can take to effectively insure their assets and gain trust. Like I mentioned before, no two clients are the same. Remember, you may already have a business plan or goals for your business. By connecting the mental aspect, you will begin to connect the dots and have everything you will need to grow.

In my experience in the insurance business, I have learned that taking a realistic approach to your surroundings and understanding them is very important. However, it is a slippery slope. I say this because once you understand your surroundings, you cannot spend time trying to change them to conform to what is comfortable to you. It doesn't work that way. This is where being realistic is key. If you are consistently encountering a negative client, you must take the time to understand what has caused this negativity or perception about our business. Face value is something we will talk about. It's not only a life insurance term but a term that also tells us that "it is what it is." Think about it. How many times in your life have you been able to snap your fingers and automatically change a situation to your favor? Not very often, I presume. There are so many different elements in the insurance business, one would be crazy to think they could do the same with *every* single scenario.

Once we have identified why your clients have developed a negative perception of our business over the years, we will focus on providing solutions to change the culture of our business, thus changing their negative perceptions. We definitely do not want to be perceived as wolves in suites, but sadly it does happen—a lot. Yes, there are wolves all around us. However, the wolf is not always bad or malicious. The wolf has always been revered as an animal that runs in a pack. Here is where this requires a little thought. A wolf can be a guardian that provides security and protection to its family, a leader. On the hand, there is the analogy that some wolves get greedy and do little to nothing to provide protection for their families and care nothing about helping others, just themselves. Are there wolves in this industry? Yes, there are; some are good, and some are not so good. You have to decide which side of the fence you will be on. Will you join the perpetual pack that has done nothing for advancing our business in a positive way? Or will you be a lone wolf and an agent of change that starts impacting lives and changing clients' negative perceptions of the insurance industry? Here again, it will do you no good to spend all your time dissecting things you cannot change. Gaining an understanding of how you will impact others in a positive manner is the key in growing as an agent and as a person.

In order to effectively grasp this concept, I will divide this idea into three specific sections that I believe would be the most effective to broaden your mental preparation about this business: the client, the competition, and you. I will use different scenarios and tie them into different aspects of the insurance business and provide insight on how a premeditated thought process will benefit you and help you better serve your clients. These scenarios will be specific to certain insurance products and provide examples of how analyzing your clients' situation beforehand will assist you in writing business. I know all of you are knowledgeable with your products and policies. Here again, this is not about your product knowledge. It is about dialing in a sort of psychology that will help you predetermine how you can serve your clients better, understand what kind of impact your competition is having in the marketplace, and (most importantly) positively conforming mentally to what you are being presented in your perspective market to write more business and become a solid person of positive impact. The goal here is to know what to expect with the insurance business and understand why there might be some negative preconceived notions attached to it. Once you know this, you can move toward changing the stagnant culture and providing solutions for client heartburns that you uncover and initiating real change. We are going to make it make sense.

The Client

CHAPTER ONE

Client Perception

I feel it is absolutely paramount to understand the perception of the majority of the clients that you will deal with on a daily basis. I believe the general consensus for most people is that the insurance industry is only out to make money and really not take a vested interest in the specific needs that someone requires. Most people in the general population are not familiar with the insurance business because it is not what they do for a living. This can cause a sense of insecurity with your client because, in their mind, they are thinking that they do not know enough about these policies to know if they are adequately covered.

The general public will tend to unfairly judge you and your business based upon experiences that they have been through along the way when dealing with other insurance companies/agents. Insurance has been around for hundreds of years and has often been depicted as a greedy industry. How many times have you spoken to someone you know who has continuously complained about how their insurance company/agent screwed them out of a claim or keeps going up in premium? We hear it all the time even before we got into the industry. So in a roundabout way, the odds are sometimes against you before you even meet with the client. Why? This all adds up to previous experiences your client has faced in the past.

What we need to understand is that this is not the client's fault. It does not matter how negative their attitude is about insurance when you first sit down with them. What matters is that, typically, this is a culmination of years and years of negative experiences that the client has gone through and is now dumping all of it on your desk before one word is even spoken. In their eyes, you are already a wolf, and not the good kind. It is important to analyze this ordeal. Think about that restaurant that you ate at years and years ago that you refuse to go back to. The service was terrible, the food was dry, and no one seemed to care when you voiced your opinion at the end. Obviously you never voice your opinion at the beginning because you risk getting your food spat in, but you get the picture. This type of experience tends to stay with people for a very long time. Is it fair? Let's say this experience was at a chain restaurant with multiple locations in your city. Does that mean you will never eat at that specific location or never eat at any of those locations? So in thinking about this, you are putting yourself in your client's shoes already.

What we need to recognize about this analogy is that previous negative experiences stay in our psychoanalysis for a very long time. Think about that person that you were absolutely crazy about in college. You tried and worked so hard to get their attention and score at least dinner. Then it finally happened. You are finally sitting across the table from this person that you have been infatuated with for years. You know what kind of person you are and what you bring to the table. They do not, however. As the night goes on, you see your chances of developing a relationship with this person slowly diminish because of their previous relationship experience. Is this your fault? Absolutely not. Is it fair? No. This person may have dated for years and fallen into the same negative experience over and over again. Guess what happens at that point? They become guarded. All of a sudden, the defense mechanisms fly at your head like an intense game of dodgeball. This person's perception of you is already negative because of experiences that have nothing to do with you.

The word *reputation* definitely comes to mind. Any insurance agent out there will develop a reputation to the general public very quickly. Why? Well, it is very simple. People talk. In an industry that is as highly competitive as insurance, people are constantly keeping the meter running by shopping around and looking for the best deal.

Remember, we are still talking about the client's perception about the industry, not you.

How many of us are just elated when it is time to go buy a used car? We, as intuitive creatures, are already expecting to be placed in a high-pressure sales situation that could only end up with us driving home a less-than-desirable vehicle. How about when someone rings your doorbell at eight at night trying to sell you a magazine subscription? We already have a predetermined notion that these situations are going to be negative and high pressure. Is that fair to the person that is trying to make a living at their craft? Would it be fair to you if the shoe was on the other foot? What happens is that this puts you into a situation where you will have to overcome a client's predetermined notion that you will continue the status quo that gave them the negative perception to begin with. Life experiences are what gives us our perception of certain entities.

I sometimes look at the perception of the insurance industry as a steady-moving stream. The current is always flowing in the same direction at an even pace. Our clients, and their experiences, are who create this stream. This is a one-dimensional take on the insurance industry in which the direction of our business is guided by less-than-favorable perception. It flows one direction. Once we, as agents, decide to jump into the business, it is very easy to let the current take us into that direction that was created by perception. As agents, we must identify with the fact that this stream was created and is here to stay. We must also understand that jumping in and letting the current take us in that one dimensional direction is an insurance career killer. We must learn to break the monotony of the one dimensional status quo. It is the history of how business has been conducted all these years that has created the status quo after all.

I remember early in my career I was sitting in my office doing paperwork. Right next door was a young lady that was a new hire. Her name was Shelly. She was very young, twenty-three years old, and right out of college. She had a great sense of humor and was always upbeat and positive. I remember thinking to myself, *Man, if she can get her business started in the right direction now, there is no telling how much money she will be making in twenty years.* Most agents that get started when they are young simply do not realize the earning potential that is staring right back at them. We had floor duty once a week where we would take calls or walk in new business. Right after lunch, the secretary buzzed into Shelly's office and informed her that she had someone in the lobby that was interested in an auto insurance quote. Shelly wasn't the type of person that would waste any time with potential new business. From my office, I had a direct line of sight to the doorway of her office. The gentleman that she greeted and was escorting into her office was in his mid- to uppersixties and looked to be in the agricultural business. I remember the look on his face when they first shook hands. It was a look of uncertainty. Right away, this man's perception of Shelly was one of uncertainty. Maybe it was because she was young. Whatever the reason was, he was already guarded. They sat down, and before she could get a word out, the man says, "Listen, I have been dealing with insurance companies for forty-five years. I have seen and heard it all. Hell, all insurance companies are the same. They squeeze as much money out of you as possible, and then when you need them the most, they tuck their tails between their legs and haul ass for the hills. I'll save you a lot of time here. Just get me some numbers, and I will compare them to the dozen that I already have, please." I remember the look on her face. It was one of shock and surprise. It was at that moment that I realized that being mentally prepared for the perceptions of my clients was absolutely crucial.

Shelly did nothing wrong. She just wasn't prepared to hear that kind of take on the insurance business from the eyes of an elderly gentleman who had been dealing with them for decades. However, I will guarantee you that going forward, she was a little more guarded with her appointments. You see, that is the problem. When you have an encounter like this and you are not mentally prepared, it could make you guarded as well. You are now guarded, and your potential client is now guarded, and this leaves no room for authentic bridge gaping. The primary goal is to get to know your client and build trust. How can trust be created when there is a gigantic wall in between the both of you before you even get started?

So what can you do when this negative perception of your insurance business is right in front of you? You have already been dubbed a wolf of insurance, and you haven't even had the opportunity to prove anyone wrong. Insurance is a wildly competitive industry, and you are looking to break the mold and move in a direction that is unconventional in a positive sense.

The first step in overcoming these predetermined perceptions is acceptance. You *have* to understand that insurance has been around for many years and these perceptions that your potential clients own have been cultivated by various encounters that have not one thing to do with you. Plain and simple, it's not your fault. However, you are set with the task of dealing with it when you are visiting with a potential client. I know it can be difficult with the notion that you are stepping into an industry that may have a negative reputation. This is where you come to terms with it and develop ways to use this to your advantage.

Accepting your potential client's perception is only the tip of the iceberg. What, did I say that you can take a client's negative perception of the insurance business and use it to your advantage? I promise you that I am not on drugs. Yes, I did say that. I am suggesting taking a negative scenario and using it to grow your business. We have all heard people complaining about how insurance companies have left a bad taste in their mouth for years. It is important in this case to know what exactly has been this client's heartburns for all these years. Accept the fact that they have a preconceived notion and move forward to providing the solution. As long as I have been in the insurance business, I can say that a cheaper rate does not always fix the problem. You have to dig deeper than that. You have to train yourself to become a better listener. These clients have these notions because no one in their past has taken the time to really listen to their concerns and provide viable solutions. It would be very easy to just quote an auto insurance policy for a customer and let rate put a bandage on the problem. You may earn the business that way, but in the long run, it will more than likely not stick. You have jumped in the stream and let the current take you in the same direction. You have now become a part of the problem.

Many of us love the insurance business because of the residual income that can be built over the course of one's career. It is one of the only businesses I know of that you can literally make money every night at midnight when a policy renews. The meter is always running. However, it can also be a revolving door. Insurance markets are designed to be competitive. When a client is dealing with an agent who perpetuates status quo cycle, the client's loyalty will be in question. What happens in this case is that the client will turn into a jumper. You've heard that term, right? The jumper is one that shops around at renewal on a consistent basis because they have determined that you are no different than any agent that they have dealt with in the past. So you see, a client's perception can have a direct effect on your growth.

Now that we have established acceptance, let us move forward to figure out exactly what has tainted your client's perception all these years. I mentioned before that listening to your clients is absolutely crucial. After all, a client's perception could have been created because their insurance agent really did not have time to hear about them and their family. "Well, all my agent cares about is making money off of me!" he may say. Or "I have asked my agent to help me review my policies for years now with no success." If you listen long enough to a prospective client, they will tell you everything you want to know about what they are looking for in an agent. The baffling thing about it is that nine times out of ten, their previous heartburns are very minor in nature. Being able to identify that a client's position about your industry needs to change is a start in the right direction.

Let's go back to Shelly for a second. She had her blinders on coming into the insurance business, and she saw firsthand how other agents have paved the way for this negative thought process with her client. What was her client looking for? Her client was looking for pure authenticity. Clients that are guarded because of previous experiences want to be able to trust their representative. After all, they have worked their entire lives accumulating their assets and are yearning for someone to take a vested interest in taking care of them. When someone comes into your office who has obviously been scorned, listen to everything they have to say. Ask questions about their families and life. Get to know them on a more intimate level. I understand that time is money, but the more time you spend with your clients listening to their story, the easier it will be for them to be unguarded with you going forward. Clients do not want to talk about you. They absolutely want to talk about them and their success stories. It is what is important to them. Shelly could've initiated this dialect by agreeing with the gentleman on all his previous complaints. However, in order to agree with a client who has preconceived negative notions, you have to understand where they are coming from. You have to understand that you are here to break that mold and become an insurance agent that is not going to follow the footsteps of everyone that has made the client bitter.

You will hear over and over in your career people talking negatively about insurance companies and agents. I believe that agents sometimes suffer from the cookie-cutter syndrome. This is simply where an agent figures that sustaining a decent career means doing what so many have done in the past. We all know of an agent that believes that success happens when you establish yourself as the alpha wolf in the market place and stomp on anyone or anything that gets in the way. Are some of these agents successful? Sure, they can be— for now. As an agent of insurance, accepting there are agents out there that follow this creed is the beginning to making a positive impact and changing the status quo. An insurance agent must also understand that this kind of practice is what has made their clients weary of the insurance industry all together.

The point that needs to be made here is this:

1. Your clients may have a preconceived perception about insurance and you even if they have never met you.
2. It is not your fault.
3. It is not your client's fault.
4. Accept these notions and move forward to finding a solution to your client's needs no matter what line of business you are in.

You cannot change years and years of process. It is what it is. Your clients will come into your office expecting the very same treatment from you that they have been getting in the past. This particular chapter is all about accepting this fact as a part of what you will deal with throughout your career. Insurance isn't typically an industry that gets impacted negatively by fluctuations in the economy. I am not saying it doesn't happen. What I am saying is that some agents may feel more comfortable with the status quo because they know that the general public will seek them out for insurance on things they need. This is absolutely what contributes to your client's perception on insurance agents and the insurance industry all together. Come to terms with this, turn the page, and be prepared to make your client's day by *not* perpetuating the cycle.

CHAPTER TWO

Centers of Influence

I think it is a common misconception to most who venture into the insurance business that clients are those that only buy insurance. Most that begin their career in the insurance business gravitate toward doing business with those that they know exclusively i.e., family, friends, etc. While tapping those you know to write insurance is an excellent practice to jump start your business, it is imperative to understand that there is an alternative market of clients just waiting for you—centers of influence.

Once you jump-start your business with walk-in clients, family, and friends, condition your mind to look into entities that can generate referral business for you. These centers of influence are typically businesses that rely on insurance companies to carry out their particular service. The really good thing about these businesses is that they are almost always in the sales industry as well. Be prepared to form a partnership with these entities. The most common centers of influence that you will encounter include, but aren't limited to, auto dealers, mortgage lenders, roofing companies, home builders, bank lenders, and realtors.

The biggest element to understand when forming a partnership with a center of influence is that the level of service you provide them is a reflection of the service they provide their clients as well. Let's take the mortgage lender as an example of this. Every day people in our country make the decision to buy a new home and turn to mortgage lenders to finance the purchase for them. Just like with insurance, there is an underwriting process in mortgage lending. This begins with the preapproval for the loan. Most people who get preapproved will then take the next step to getting a quote for the purchase of the home. This will include information on the taxes, purchase price, down payment amount, and also annual insurance premium. That's right. So now you see where I am going with this.

Please understand that there are some home buyers that will contact their auto insurance agent for a homeowner's insurance quote the first chance they get. That is completely all right, because that might be you! On the other side of the coin, most first-time home buyers will directly ask the mortgage lender who they recommend for house insurance. Now it is all starting to fall together, isn't it? Now you are starting to see the importance of conditioning your mind into understanding how clients are all around us at all times!

Earlier I mentioned that we, as insurance agents, could be a direct reflection of the service that these centers of influence provide. Well, that is very true in the case of the mortgage lender. Let's say, for example, a lender refers a potential home-buyer client to an agent for a quote on house insurance. Let's say the agent shoots the home buyer a quote, and he commits to buying the policy. At this point in time, after learning that their client has committed to the house insurance quote, they will send the insurance agent a hazard insurance request form. This form will request a binder of coverage on the house insurance that their client elected. Here is where I make my point. In order for the underwriting process to commence, this binder has to be sent to the lender (by the agent) as soon as possible. The longer it takes the agent to send the binder to the lender, the longer it takes to get their client moving toward buying and moving into their home. If an agent subsequently drags their feet on supplying the binder to the lender, it could hold up production. They have to have this information in order for their client to close on their new home. It is very possible for the buyer's closing date to be postponed for weeks if the agent does not get the insurance binder back to the lender in a timely manner. It all has to be fluid. I would rather be locked in a cage with a rabid wolf than be the reason buyers have to wait to get into their new home, especially if they have already sold their previous home or terminated their rental lease. What does this mean? It means they will have to come out of pocket for a hotel room or go stay with family or friends until they can finally close—all because of you. You get the picture.

I use the scenario of the mortgage lender because it is a perfect example of my point. You see, all mortgage lenders want is a smooth transaction between you and them. The smoother you are, the smoother they are. The ideology behind this is to always be prepared to come through for your referral sources. They need you in order to carry out their business. So in a roundabout way, you are a reflection of the services that they provide. You have to understand how much of a crapshoot this may be for another business. They can be fantastically proficient on their side of the craft. Once they reach the point of their process that requires an insurance agent, this is when they place themselves at the mercy of others. We must stop and understand how difficult and nerve racking this may be for a business. I visualize the sprint relay. There are four legs to the four-by-four-hundred sprint relay. Once the sprinter hands off that baton, he or she has done all they can do up to that point. There are no do overs. All they can do is perform the best they can and hope that the person running the next leg of the race can help maintain the momentum. The end result of the race will include all parties involved. The goal is now achieved.

There is nothing that a business (center of influence) wants more than to establish a network with entities they need to conduct their own business. This creates credibility for that particular business. As an insurance agent, you have to be aware of what you are providing these centers of influence. It is your leg of the relay. What are you providing? You are providing value. Not only have you gained a client by writing insurance for them, but you have also gained another client in your center of influence. You have now provided positive value to two different clients. You are now a person of influence as well.

Condition your mind to understand that you have the ability to make someone's life better by what you do. I understand that this might seem a little far-fetched, but it is not. These centers of influence have reached out to you to aide them in helping someone potentially change their life. I used the example of the mortgage lender. Picture when you bought your first home. This may be an easier road for others. There is no telling how much someone has gone through in order to complete their goal of homeownership. Working multiple jobs, commuting a long way for more pay, living with parents to save money, etc. Perhaps someone has just arrived from doing several tours in the military. You must understand that you are touching lives here.

Every day, thousands of teenagers get their driver's licenses. There are two sides of the coin here. There is the parent that dreads this because they are seeing their child turn into a young adult who is now old enough to operate a motor vehicle. The other side is the teenager who is ridiculously elated because they will now have the ability to operate a motor vehicle and initiate their social status. Either which way you look at it, the idea of security is of the upmost importance for the parent. They want to make sure their child is adequately covered at all times. When that dealership calls upon you to refer an auto insurance quote for this client, it isn't about getting wet ink on a contract and collecting your money. You are now responsible for making sure that someone's child (their most pride and joy) is insured fully to the client's specifications. You have helped a dealership with a process that is life changing. In doing this, you have become a part of a network in which the cycle will continue to repeat itself so long as you are upholding your end of the sprint relay. A lot of times, dealerships will not let someone leave the parking lot (in their new purchase) until insurance has been bound and proof of coverage has been complete. Do you see the similarities with the auto dealer and the mortgage lender? The car salesman has now become your client, and your service is a direct reflection of the experience that their client will have when buying a vehicle. The relationship is symbiotic.

The concept of forming a partnership with outside businesses really doesn't dawn on an aspiring insurance agent. As insurance agents, we must dig a little deeper into the process to gain a complete understanding of how it all works. Waiting at your office for walk-in business is only a fraction of a fraction of what is out there for you. Most centers of influence that you will encounter exists to help others bring a desire to fruition. For the most part, the general public can see buying a house or a car as a stressful ordeal. Stop right there. Picture yourself at your office seeing a client pull up with a brand-new car for their sixteen-year-old. The hard part and all the legwork is already over. You weren't there for all that. I believe there are times when agents take this for granted. Your client comes in, then you quote the insurance and issue the policy. After you issue them a proof of insurance, your job is done, right?

Being involved in the process can really put things into perspective for an agent. If you allow yourself to open your heart to the people you serve, it will give you a more in-depth understanding of what it is you really do. Our centers of influence are the ones that help people with their dreams and goals. Why not be a part of that? Do we, as agents, only need to be involved when (by chance) someone pulls up to our office to actually buy insurance? In the case of the mortgage lender, you actually have to fulfill your end of the bargain in order for the buyer of a home to get their loan. Get involved with your centers of influence. Become a part of their process and make it easier for them to carry out their duties.

One thing that you will notice very quickly in the insurance business is that your centers of influence are very much tightly knit. One of the fundamental aspects of the center of influence is networking. As an insurance agent, you may get invited to a meeting for the Association of Realtors. What an awesome opportunity this is to network. At one of these functions, you will encounter realtors, home builders, mortgage lenders, bankers, contractors, and the list goes on and on. Tread very carefully, however. It isn't enough to attend these gatherings and just hand out cards. If you want to avoid the label of the insurance wolf, you have to take it a step further than just spraying your cards around the room. If you shake hands with someone and automatically slap a card in their hand right after, then they're going to be thinking, *Well, here's another jackass insurance agent that won't let me get a word in, but yes, let's hear all about you.*

25

That's right. These preconceived notions about insurance agents that we spoke of earlier rears its ugly face again. I promise you, if you light that fuse, it will blow up in your face and you will be dubbed a wolf for much of the foreseeable future. Why? Well, it's because these preconceived notions have been around for many years, and you are doing nothing to change it. Instead, yet again, you have jumped into the perpetual stream and have let the current take you along with years of sustained negative opinions. You have to turn the tide dammit! You have to understand that this is what everyone expects to happen when they encounter an insurance agent, especially a new one! Instead, when you are shaking hands with a center of influence, do everything you can to get to know them and their business. If you listen to them long enough, you will learn more about the way they conduct their business and inevitably learn what turns them off and on with dealing with insurance agents. I understand it is very difficult earning trust with just an introduction or two. However, look at it this way. If you are a realtor and meet an insurance agent that isn't going on and on about themselves, you automatically know there is something different about them. That is how you change perceptions. You give them something that is out of the ordinary. Don't spend time talking about yourself and all of your accomplishments. Instead, ask your centers of influence about their accomplishments and what is important to them. Let them know you're not there to just beat referral business out of them. Become genuinely interested in the other person. What happens next? *You* become a person who has influenced change. You have changed the mentality of people that you have encountered by not being overly self-absorbed, and in turn, you have created a different path for your centers of influence to travel down.

Centers of influence and general clients can be very similar in one basic way: they will both spread the word about you. Whether it is positive or negative word is completely up to you. I have emphasized heavily about going against the grain and creating a mechanism of change. You absolutely want to establish yourself as someone that is consistent in the way you do business. Taking a vested interest in the other person can be difficult for someone who is anxious to get their business off the ground. The key here is patience. Now, I will be honest. Patience is something that I have struggled with my entire career. As a young, ambitious agent, I was ready to hit the ground running and conquer every goal that I bestowed upon myself. I needed to take a step back and really put into perspective why I was in this business. The insurance business can humble you real quick. If you are only in it for yourself and are only in it for monetary gain, you've lost the battle before even setting foot on the field.

If you are consistent in the way you help your centers of influence, word will catch on that you are indeed a different breed of agent. Oftentimes, centers of influence will take the "lesser of all evils" approach. Let me explain what this is. Similar to your walk-in clients, centers of influence will callous over after years and years of dealing with insurance agents that do not consistently deliver. These business will experience hundreds of insurance agents drop by their offices to drop off business cards and ask for referral business. It is a very monotonous practice that will do nothing but produce the same preconceived notions about the insurance industry in its entirety. As a result of this practice, centers of influence will literally choose an agent out of a sea of mediocre inventory that does the best worst job. It is literally the definition of insanity. It is absolutely not their fault though. They are just simply dealing with a lack of viable options and forcing themselves to select someone who they can get by with.

Why should this be the case? As insurance agents, we, aside from knowing what to expect, need to raise the bar. We know that our centers of influence can absolutely be essential in helping us grow our business. Let's put them first. Show them that they matter to you and you are willing to partner with them in order to help them carry out their task of touching lives. We mentioned consistency earlier. Consistency will build trust. If the mortgage lender knows that you are committed to getting them all the necessary paperwork in order for them to complete their task, the more likely they will be to recommend you to their client base. This equals referrals, and referrals equals growth. Remember, this all starts with recognizing the preconceived perception and committing yourself to be an agent—an agent of change.

CHAPTER THREE

Keeping it Simple

Whether you are in the insurance business already or are in the process of, you are probably well aware of the immense amount of studying and learning you have to do. Not only do you have to pass your state licensing exam for your license(s), but you also have to begin the process of learning everything about your company and its products. It doesn't stop there. You have to get to know your underwriters, policy service representatives, and all your company's support staff. If you decide not to become a captive agent and go independent, this may get a little more difficult because you will have to get acquainted with all the companies that you decide to get appointed with. This will definitely take time.

Insurance agents are constantly learning. Product knowledge is essential and must be a priority because it is essential before you venture out to study your market and clients. The point that I make here is that the general public will have no idea of everything you have gone through in order to become a professional in the insurance business. The constant hours of studying for your exams, products, and every step in between does not (and will not) even dawn on your client base. Why would it? Your clients are not insurance experts—you are.

Having said that, it brings me to one of the most important and fundamental aspects of the insurance business: keep it simple! Becoming an expert in the insurance business takes time. Do not try and tread the deeper waters right out of the block. Your clients are going to want reassurance that you are protecting their assets and interests. Take the step ladder approach and start from the bottom up. On a property and casualty basis, here is an example:

Rung 5: Commercial
Rung 4: Umbrella Liability
Rung 3: Inland Marine
Rung 2: Home and Renters Insurance
Rung 1: Auto insurance

Using the ladder approach is important because it gives you a progressive example on how to get well versed in lines that typically end up being the nucleus of your business. In the case of property and casualty, auto and property insurance is a good place to start by keeping it simple. This is typically what the normal consumer seeks out first in insurance. Becoming an expert in these lines of business first will help build your confidence and help you gain more exposure in that particular arena. You have to crawl before you walk.

Since your client base normally isn't insurance savvy, keeping it simple is a definite way to gain their confidence as well. Remember, as I mentioned before, the general public will know next to nothing about insurance. They will lean on you for support, advice, and peace of mind. For this reason, keeping it simple with the lines of business you can provide is crucial because it will limit the complexity in the situations you will put yourself in before testing out deeper waters. Now, I am not saying that you will never run into clients that will have more questions than the average bear. This is why I touched on product knowledge earlier. Someone may ask you specifics of different endorsements on their homeowner's policy or auto policy. They could be testing your product knowledge, or they could be very meticulous about certain aspects of that insurance policy.

I really do believe that most of the clients that present themselves to you will not grill you every time they see you. They want a basic understanding of their policy and want to move on. Be careful here, though. Seeing this trend in clients can actually promote a plateau effect in which the agent will not seek to progress in learning more about their products. This falls right back into the preconceived notions that clients have about insurance agents that we have been discussing in the previous two chapters.

Let's say that you are in the life insurance business. We all know that there are vast amounts of life insurance available to the public. There are life insurance products to secure families, business interests, estate taxes, etc. It does not matter how diverse your life insurance portfolio is; you can never go wrong with keeping it simple for your clients at the beginning. Perhaps you may target families that will entail writing more term and whole life products. Once you are well versed in term and whole life, you can segue into more complicated lines of business. If you choose to keep your business simple at first, you will inevitably become more of an expert because you have isolated specific products and studied them more in depth. This is what the general client needs. You will be able to explain term and whole life insurance to a family with confidence. You can educate them and help them understand the value of protecting their family with the right coverage. As a general rule, the public tends to think about life insurance in a morbid way. You can take this opportunity to show them how whole life products can actually help them build a nest egg for future financial use. Let's move their perceptions about life insurance and show them that life insurance isn't about the people that pass—it's about the people that live.

I firmly believe that keeping it simple can actually help you gain the product knowledge you need to effectively serve your clients. Why? This is because you have chosen to become an expert in what you will believe to be the foundation of your business. You start on the first rung and climb as time goes by. There is nothing wrong with sticking to the basics at first and then swinging for the fence later. After all, the clientele that you will be dealing with at first will stem from the basics, i.e., home, auto, and life insurance. Take the time to explain these fundamental policies in depth to your clients. Remember that they do not do this for a living. You are the expert, not them. This is where you change the game. Most of our clients, due to misappropriated perception, just are not used to an agent sitting with them and explaining their policies in depth.

Just because you are keeping it simple at first does not mean that more complicated lines of business will not manifest itself before you. This is where much caution needs to be taken. Let's say you are a new agent and you are wrapping up an auto insurance policy for some clients. Upon talking to them, you discover that they own a couple of grocery stores in the community. Now, your normal instinct will be to ask them about their businesses and inquire about their commercial insurance. That is your job! This is the only way you are going to grow. Never miss an opportunity to expand. In situations like this, please make sure that you have the proper support system and guidance to help you with business you are not too familiar with. This will happen. I have learned over the years help is just a phone call away. Insurance companies that appoint you are chock-full of agent support systems that are there to assist you in issuing business. Eventually, with repetition, climbing the ladder will be a reality, and you will start to see your knowledge of this business expand tremendously.

Knowledge is what your clients are seeking from you. Here again, I believe that the best way to give them what they need is to start from the bottom and work your way up the rungs. A client can sense incompetence a mile away. It does happen. The lack of confidence with an insurance policy will create doubt with your client base that will, inevitably, end up with retention problems and continued jumpers. There is no telling how broad your portfolio will be. I have seen, too many times, agents trying to bite off more than they can chew in regard to writing policies. What your clients are looking for is someone that is going to be honest and truthful about what they know and don't know.

Clients can be very unpredictable at what they will throw at you. There are clients out there that will show up at your office to insure their home and auto. What they will not tell you is that they are successful business owners and have twenty million dollars in assets. Perhaps they have already placed their commercial business with someone else who specializes in commercial insurance. There is a reason they have split their business this way. Perhaps they have no confidence in their personal lines agent to insurance their commercial business. Perhaps it is the other way around. What a terrible inconvenience for the client. There is nothing worse for a client than to have multiple lines of insurance scattered around the community with different companies. There is much to be said about an insurance agent who has *all* of a client's lines of business under one roof. This is the ultimate goal, but I am telling you, this is not going to happen three months into your career when you have hungry hippo syndrome and are trying to swallow every bit of business that you see in the distance. This is where the client will see what you do not want them to see—incompetence. Take your time with your business. Keeping it simple at first will help you become more knowledgeable about your core business.

We all know NASA. NASA is an organization that has literally been defying the laws of physics for many years. The technology that is used at NASA to carry out its agenda is untouchable. We are talking about the world's most intelligent men and women working in a cohesive unit to accomplish the unfathomable. I picture an assembly line of MIT graduates lined up at NASA's gates ready to add to the already-impeccable team of geniuses. It is really quite fascinating to think about everything they have done and the minds that have contributed to its success. From putting men on the moon to constructing mobile probes to gather data on Mars, NASA continues to be the foremost institution of scientific advancement. It is safe to say that NASA does not keep things simple. Can you imagine the time and research that goes into one single solitary project?

In regard to NASA, I am reminded of a story that I heard once on television. I do not know if the story was true, but I found it quite humorous, and it is a great example of complicated versus simplicity. NASA, for many years, has been sending astronauts into space for a variety of different reasons. The astronauts that stay months at a time at the international space station are required to gather data and carry out many responsibilities that NASA requests. Upon gathering data, NASA comes to the conclusion that they need to invent a pen that would effectively write (in ink) at zero gravity. So they commission a team of engineers (probably MIT alum) to come up with such a design. They work diligently for months to come up with this zero-gravity pen. They spend many hours and many tax dollars until they finally come up with the ultimate design. The engineers run through the ranks of NASA until it is finally approved for construction. The team gathers all their blueprints and data and begin building this pen that is set to defy all odds and write in space.

Almost a year later, a prototype is constructed. The many months of research and testing on the pen has now turned into a year. One year it takes the team to come up with this complicated design that will write at zero gravity. That is what NASA does. They take the long way and spend millions of dollars to invent this pen to carry out the task of writing down data in space. They recruit the best of the best and the most gifted engineers at NASA to spearhead this project.

The day has come, and it is time to relieve the astronaut at the space station with another one. The countdown begins, and off the pen goes. Into the cosmos to see if the young geniuses have succeeded in their invention. The new astronaut arrives, with the pen in hand, and proceeds to test out the gadget to see if it works. Alas, a success it is! NASA has defied all odds and actually has created a pen that will write in zero gravity. The elite team of engineers has succeeded in all their glory. What a huge victory for NASA and the United States of America! Russia, in the same scenario, just uses a pencil...

In the insurance business, it is so easy to overcomplicate things. What you need to realize is that you can still get from point A to Z whether you take the simple route or the complicated one. I think the example of the zero-gravity pen is a great example of this. NASA completed the goal of recording data in outer space. Whether it was simple or complicated was up to them. In your case, it will be up to your client. Your client already believes that insurance is cumbersome and complicated. Remember, they do not do this for a living. Think about when you were in college or high school. You were sitting in physiology class, and the instructor is going a hundred miles an hour. You are breaking your wrist trying to write down as many notes as you can so you can study later only to realize you are more confused later than you were in the classroom. The instructor is the expert and knows the subject like the back of his or her hand. It's only when you decide to spend time later going over the information at your own pace or elect to get a tutor to simplify the subject to your specification that things fall into focus.

As an insurance agent, simplifying the subject and making sure the client understands the policy is the way to go. It is all starting to land in perspective. By keeping it simple, you gain knowledge on the fundamental aspects of the business and will be able to convey the information to your client with confidence. This will erase the client's preconceived notion that you will automatically overcomplicate everything insurance related without taking into account that they are not experts on the topic. Slow it down a bit. Reassure your clientele that you are willing to make it make sense for them. Your portfolio is not going anywhere. Those products will be at your disposal from the first day you are appointed on. Become well versed on the core products (home, auto, life), and then when you have gained your client's trust, you will be confident enough to tread the deeper waters with more complicated lines of business.

The idea of keeping your process simple can be very much effective with your centers of influence as well. Remember, the majority of these centers of influence already conduct business that will be pertinent to the lines of business that you will be trying to become well versed at in order to keep things simple. Home and auto insurance tend to be the lines of business that aspiring agents commence their businesses on. This is a good thing. In the property and casualty realm, home and auto insurance are the lines of business that serve as a segue into other complicated lines of business. Keeping things simple will be an effective way to take care of your referral sources. Stay on task. If a mortgage lender is asking for a property binder after their client has accepted your quote for homeowner's insurance, be fundamentally sound and get them the paperwork as soon as possible. Don't try and get fancy.

Tim Duncan, now retired, was perhaps one of the greatest power forwards in NBA history. His nickname was Mr. Fundamental. How many times did you see him get fancy with his game? How many times did you get the impression that he played the game to razzle and dazzle instead of get the job at hand done? No, he made a name for himself by sticking to the fundamentals of the game. He kept it simple, didn't he? This is why he almost always got the ball during clutch situations. If the Spurs were down by one in the fourth quarter, with only nine seconds left on the clock, what do you think the plan was? Perhaps designing an inbound play that consisted of a pick to free up a three point shot? Hell no. The ball was going to Duncan. A simple pick and roll to get him the ball in the paint. He would use a fundamental jump shot off the glass and nail it almost every time. This would inevitably create the prize that we all seek—trust. Greg Popovich (center of influence) knows that giving Duncan the ball increases his chance of the ultimate goal: victory. Duncan earned this trust. He earned it by consistently using fundamentals to produce results. No flash or extra complications were needed. Get him the ball, and watch him use the most basic glass shot in the book for the score.

Use the analogy of keeping your business simple, and you will soon see that your referral sources will trust you enough to integrate you into their process. Not only this, your general clientele will see something different in you as their agent. Here again, you are breaking the mold and showing the public that you are willing to put in the work, keep things simple, and use fundamentally sound ideology to gain their trust and make them comfortable with elements they may not be well versed in.

CHAPTER FOUR

Bringing It All Together

The first two chapters of this section were closely based on perceptions that have been cultivated over the course of many years. Your clients, whether the general public or referral businesses, have become conditioned by a generic pattern that your predecessors have created. Is it your fault? No, it is not. Is it their fault? I do not believe so.

In college, I had the privilege of taking an introductory psychology class. In retrospect, I wish I had taken more. I have always been fascinated by how the human mind works. I really do believe that my fascination with the human mind has really helped me grow my business over the years. How, you ask? Well, it's simple. I take a vested interest in understanding my clients. Being mentally prepared for what the insurance business will throw at you will be a huge advantage.

In this psychology class, we studied a specific experiment that always kind of stuck with me. It was called classical conditioning. This experiment involved a variety of dogs. We all know that when a dog begins to salivate, this indicates that the dog is hungry or knows it is about to feast. The goal of the experiment was to find some sort of stimulant that would trigger salivation in the dog. The stimulant was not to be the food itself—that was the catch. For a series of sessions, the dogs were given food on a schedule. The next step was to find the stimulant. They decided to get an average bell and use it as the stimulant. So in the following sessions, they would ring the bell right before serving the dog's food. Soon, it became a trend, something the dogs expected. In the sessions to come, they continued ringing the bell but did not bring the food right away. What do you think was the result when the bell was rung? You guessed it. The dogs would begin salivating when they heard the bell because their minds were classically conditioned and they knew the sound of the bell indicated that food was coming.

Of course, I would never compare our clientele to dogs. The point I am trying to make is that your clients have been conditioned over the years to expect certain results from the average insurance agent. When it's renewal time on their policies, or it's time to shop for another insurance carrier, this conditioning doesn't usually trigger excitement or something to look forward to. It's not their fault. They are simply victims of the same old callous agenda that the status quo insurance agents have created. You have identified that there are preconceived notions by the public, you understand who your clients will be, and you are considering taking a simplistic approach to business that will build your confidence with your new products. What's next?

Now, we bring it all together. We are going to look into bridging the gaps that keep us from making those key connections with our clients. I would never call this a plan of attack. This is a plan of resolution. The key to creating a resolution for this stale pattern of business is *communication*. Communication in the insurance business will also include becoming a professional listener. I have always been a huge proponent on communication not only in business but in life in general. Just because you know that your client probably has been subject to mediocre treatment over the years does not mean that you know how or why. I can answer the why part: their previous agents were lazy, plain and simple. The wolves of insurance decided that playing a round of golf was more important than providing sincere service.

In the property and casualty business, most clients will come to you because they *need* an insurance policy. Most of the time this will be the case because they have to satisfy some sort of lien holder or financial obligation to a bank. This leads to a robotic process. The client comes in, you quote the business, and you ask them to press hard because the bottom copy is theirs. There is no substance with robotic transactions. Why? Well, because it *is* a transaction. Going to the DMV is a robotic transaction. There is limited interaction and fellowship. I can guarantee you that the general public knows exactly what to expect when visiting the DMV. You have to open the lines of communication with your clientele. Let them know that you are genuinely interested in them and everything that is important to them. Open your mind, heart, and your ears.

I mentioned earlier that if you listen long enough to a client, they will tell you everything you need to know about their previous experiences. At this point, it would definitely not hurt to ask, "So what did you find unsatisfactory about your previous carrier?" Get ready. Once you ask this question, you are subjecting yourself to hear venting that has been bottled up for many years because no one has had the decency to ask, let alone care. Embrace this. This is exactly what you want. All of a sudden, your client is telling you exactly what he has experienced over the years dealing with subpar insurance agents or companies. Take notes. Now you know what you can do to bridge the gap and make that connection.

I call these negative experiences heartburns. I am telling you that you will be amazed at how minor and minuscule these heartburns will be. I reference the mortgage lender earlier and how important it was to provide them with the hazard insurance binder after the client has accepted your quote for insurance. I also mentioned how not getting those documents to the lender could actually delay a client from completing the purchase of their home. Crazy, isn't it? Preparing a hazard binder for a lender and e-mailing (or faxing) it to them should only take minutes. How hard is it to take ten minutes out of your day to get your referral source documentation they need to complete their process? I can promise you one thing: it is definitely worth your time. These centers of influence have the ability to send you a ton of business. It is up to you to show them that things will be different.

The same holds true for your general client who is just looking for an auto insurance quote. Once you know their heartburns, you have a golden opportunity to make sure you go in the opposite direction and break the monotony of mediocre treatment. Most clients are not unreasonable. Like I mentioned before, most of the issues they have will be easily rectified. Perhaps they just want a return phone call, within a reasonable time, from their agent when they have a coverage question. Return the damn phone call as soon as you can! Maybe they want an annual review of their policies to make sure that everything is where it needs to be. Do the damn review! Going the extra mile for most clientele, in the insurance business, really isn't unreasonable at all. You just have to be willing to do that on a consistent basis.

One thing that you should be well aware of, and keep an eye out for, is the pattern of heartburns that will be evident. The longer you are in the insurance business, you will begin to encounter more and more clients on a weekly basis. I implore you to pay attention to the types of heartburns that will manifest in front of you. You will start to notice patterns as they pertain to certain lines of business. What I mean by this is that these heartburns will be significant to property insurance, auto insurance, life insurance, and so forth and so on. You may be thinking that this can get complicated and cumbersome to keep up with. If you ask me, it is quite the advantage. What you have now is a way to categorize your clients' heartburns. They won't intertwine. Different lines of insurance have different procedures and underwriting guidelines. Odds are, these heartburns will be similar as they pertain to a certain line of business. It is my opinion that this a great way to keep your "bridging the gap" process simple. There it is, folks. Keeping it simple. You just cannot go wrong with keeping it simple.

Without identifying what your client's heartburns are, you cannot effectively apply a solution. You will just continue to spin your tires and go nowhere. I really do believe that the general public has accepted the fact that the insurance business is a stale and robotic business that perpetuates long and boring processes. Sadly enough, I also believe that they feel like it is out of their control. Ladies and gentlemen, your clients should never feel this way when they step into your office. Subsequently, they will. This holds especially true when the client is looking for insurance they have to have. They are thinking, *Well, I have to have insurance on this new truck I bought. I guess I will start looking around.* They will start looking around because they feel they will get the exact same treatment because "all insurance agents are the same." Do you accept this? I sure as hell don't.

I remember years ago I had moved to a new city. It wasn't too large of a city, maybe 130,000 people or so. I had previously lived in three other towns and could never find a decent place to get my oil changed. Everywhere I went, I ran into the same terrible service that I had experienced before. The level of atrocious service ranged from unfriendly people to forgetting a key element in the oil changing process that would cause a distinct burning smell under my hood. I kid you not, it happened every single damn time! I was driving around on a Saturday about 1,500 miles overdue for an oil change and pulled into this oil and lube shop that specialized in just oil changes. They had someone waiting to guide you into the bay and direct you to keep moving forward until you were in the right position over the cellar. I got out of my truck, and I was greeted by a very nice woman who asked how she could help me. I said, "I just need an oil change, nothing more." I was kind of short with her because, in my previous experiences, I had to fight everyone off for twenty minutes because they would try to upsell me with unnecessary nonsense. "Not a problem!" she responded. She took my keys and walked me into the cleanest waiting area I had ever seen in an oil changing shop. There was a glass sliding door that I looked through to see everything they were doing. There was one technician in the cellar changing the oil, one vacuuming the inside of my truck, another one cleaning my windows, and another one checking my filters. I noticed how clean the shop was. If I had food, I could've eaten off the floor. They had the music playing, and they were all laughing and having a good time. I was there ten minutes. The lady came back to let me know my truck was ready. I was caught off guard because it was so quick. She walked me to the register, and I paid for the service. Every one of the technicians thanked me for the business, and I drove off.

I was one of those clients. Guilty as charged. I came into the shop expecting the same kind of treatment that I had been getting for years. I had a preconceived notion that this experience was going to be no different than the rest. Now, I know that the oil changing business and the insurance business are different as night and day. However, I did leave one key part out. As I was paying for the oil change, the lady asked me, "How was your experience here today?" I said, "Different... but in a good way!" She gave me a survey to fill out and return for a discount on my next oil change. So you see, they were there to pick up on heartburns just like you. Their method was a little different, but the concept was the same. They wanted to know how their service stacked up to the rest. I'm sure that upon returning the survey, they would look and see if there were any complaints and do whatever it took to make the next experience even better. This shop had broken the mold. They had changed my preconceived notion that all oil changing shops were the same. I have been getting my oil changed there for thirteen years now. Technicians have left over the years, but the atmosphere has never changed. During these thirteen years, they have increased their prices some. I can truly say that I do not care one bit.

I have said that communication is absolutely crucial in uncovering your client's heartburns. Providing solutions for these heartburns to change your client preconceived notion of the insurance business is next on the list. How do you do this? It is very simple: you follow through!

I have mentioned that if you listen long enough and care enough to ask, the client will tell you everything you need to know about how and why they have a bad taste their mouth about insurance. The reason I have preached keeping it simple is because you will have a portfolio of a variety of different insurance products at your disposal. It would be very easy to get sidetracked. By keeping it simple at first, you can concentrate on handling these heartburns one at a time. This will help keep you organized and ensure that you can focus on a more contained area of insurance. This will make your follow-through much easier.

I'm sure that there are hundreds of insurance agents out there that are fully capable of hearing the client's heartburn. The concern has been voiced. It is your job as an agent to make sure that those concerns never resurface. As I mentioned before, you would not believe how minor and ridiculous some of these heartburns may be. People are looking for agents that will go that extra mile. The funny thing is, what is a mile to the client should only be an inch to you!

Let's say you speak with a client and they open up to you about their heartburn. Come to find out, the one thing that has given them a sour taste in their mouth is the fact that their agent never returns their phone call. There are people out there that feel much more comfortable speaking to their agent as opposed to a secretary or service representative. So a client calls in and needs to speak with you. Your service rep leaves you a message to call this client back. You don't. Two weeks later, the client calls you to file a claim on their homeowner's insurance after a huge hailstorm. Upon looking at the policy, you discover that the policy had cancelled for nonpayment the previous week before. As it turns out, the client was calling you two weeks ago because the mortgage company had changed his house insurance billing from mortgage pay to customer pay. He needed to talk to you because his mortgage company told him that he would have to commence payment on his house insurance and he did not believe that's how it should work. To make a long story short, the hailstorm causes over twenty thousand dollars worth of damage on his roof alone totaling it out. Not only that, the damage from the hail stones has caused the roof to leak, and it looks like the forecast calls for more rain in the upcoming days. This is a pretty big bill to have to pay for roof repairs. Does the insured have the money? Maybe they do, maybe they don't. The point is, they shouldn't have to indemnify themselves for your mistake. Had you made one phone call back to the client to let them know how the new billing worked, you could've avoided this whole situation and saved the client a whirlwind of financial trouble. One phone call—that's it.

A large part of the reason negative preconceived notions exist is because of the lack of follow-through by agents. I can promise you this, your client will be thinking to themselves, *I do not know what is so hard about picking up the damn phone and calling someone back!* They are 100 percent right. It is ludicrous to me to think that years and years of negative perceptions were created by clients because of such minuscule things. As an aspiring agent, I feel it is important for you to understand that not only do these negative notions exist but also how easy they are to avoid.

Prepare yourself to take on these long-standing issues that have plagued the insurance industry for years. It is absolutely imperative to know that your clients have experienced subpar service, and these clients come in various entities. Whether they are general clients or high-paced realtors and mortgage lenders, they need to see that you are here to change their experiences for the absolute better. Keep your head on a swivel. By this, I mean always be on the lookout for these clients that have negative feelings about the insurance industry. Once you have made the determination, make it your priority to find the solutions. We are not interested in Band-Aids. We are looking for long-term positive change that will result in trust, confidence, and continued growth.

The Competition

CHAPTER FOUR

The Funnel Effect

How many times have you heard the expression "Know your competition"? I believe it is a useful practice. Sure, why not? However, knowing your competition goes a lot deeper than knowing who they are, where they are located, what they specialize in, etc. Sure, you can use your senses and know your competition. You can visually see your competition and hear about your competition. Segue into a more in-depth psychological understanding about your competition. After all, we have spoken all along about negative preconceived notions that your clients have about the insurance industry. Who do you think has created this trend? That's right—the competition.

Not all competition is bad. You will run into insurance agents that are willing to send the occasional lead your way. This typically will only be the case if that agent receives a request to quote a particular line of business that they do not have a market for. For example, let's say that you receive a call from XYZ insurance down the road from you. They have received a phone call to quote a general liability for an oil and gas company. However, their markets stay away from liability policies in the oil and gas industry. The agent from XYZ insurance company, whom you've met, knows that you do have a market and will send them your way. Does this happen often? Unfortunately, it does not. However, it is good to recognize that not all insurance agents are wolves in ties.

As competitive as the insurance business is, you will learn that quoting insurance has lost some of its integral substance. I will tell you what I mean by this. In any given month, there are hundreds of people that call various insurance companies for quotes in insurance. Common sense tells us that as consumers, we are conditioned to have the desire to save as much money as we can at all times. Saving money drives the competitive nature in business. Some say it's what keeps the blood in our economy flowing. Remember, though, insurance is all about building a residual income based on risk. It does nothing for any insurance agent to write everything that comes through the door. This is called the funnel effect.

The funnel effect correlates with the competitive nature of insurance and the steady flow of consumers that actively shop for cheaper rates on a consistent basis. People are already conditioned to jump from insurance company to insurance company in search of cheap rates. This is where I say that quoting insurance has lost some if its integral substance. Instead of being an agent of insurance and seeking the right coverage for the client, you become an agent of quoting. There is no substance there. Just data and numbers being entered into the system. You have to identify that this is the trend that has been created by the competition.

The funnel effect feeds off this trend. Your competition is well aware that you are in business and will do whatever it takes to take business away from you. What happens next is that insurance agents will get into the habit of lowballing every quote that comes through the door. This creates the funnel and leads to a multitude of negative things. First of all, the funnel effect takes credibility away from the agent as someone who is genuinely interested in the client's needs. At this point, it is all about the money and all about securing the business. Henceforth, the client will (once again) gain that perspective of an insurance agent only interested in money, a wolf of insurance. Remember, this is *exactly* what the client expects from you. Change the culture! Secondly, the funnel effect constitutes writing every piece of business in sight without effectively examining the risk. What does this matter? It keeps your client playing musical chairs with rates and, as a result, keeps you on the perpetual treadmill, never moving forward to grow your business. You have now become a part of the very issue that I am asking you to identify and provide solutions for. Lastly, by giving into the funnel effect, you fail to accept your role as a risk manager. Writing business on everything without assessing the risk can result in higher claims. Higher claims result in higher premiums. You are literally chasing your tail at this point. There is no progression. You will not grow.

This is where I call you to action. Do not be a funnel effect agent of insurance. Change the culture and let your clients know that you do care about them and their needs. Sure, you can funnel the business in, lowball the rates, and increase your subsequent pay. But it will not last. In insurance, you cannot conduct business day by day. You must look at the big picture down the road. Taking a vested interest in your client will break the mold and build trust. You may have to turn down business that appear to be elevated risks. That is a part of the business. These are actual trends in the business. They are what can create negative notions about the insurance industry. Why wouldn't they? Do not get caught contributing to the funnel effect way of conducting business; you will not be able to afford it.

One thing that is crucial to identifying the funnel effect is to examine your client's existing policies. Just running them a quote for insurance is not enough. I have tossed the term *lowballing* a couple of times already. Get in the habit of examining your client's existing insurance policies, and you will see just how much of a problem low-balling can be. The competition will sometimes get into the habit of running quotes with just basic coverage in order to get the business through lower premiums. It happens all the time. This is a dangerous and very selfish practice. Think about it. You have a client that you have written a house insurance policy on their $300,000 home. On the policy, you have all the endorsements you feel will adequately cover their beautiful house for a premium of $2,800 per year. You must realize, as an agent, how easy it is for the competition to look at this policy and know exactly what to do to lower the premiums to $2,000 per year. Now, I am not saying this will happen all the time and that all your competition will subscribe to this behavior. Wolves may be present, but not all the time. A competitor can requote this business, shave endorsements, convince the client they don't need them, and take the business from you for a cheaper premium.

These kinds of practices can result in catastrophic losses, as well as lawsuits and errors and omission claims. There is nothing good about combining the funnel effect and lowballing practices. Being thorough with your clients is the key. One complaint you will hear from time to time is that the agent just had the client sign the contract and gave vague details about the policy itself. This happens with the funnel effect all the time. As long as the competition is writing business and cashing a paycheck, there is little concern for the well-being of the client and their families.

Something that I have noticed with the funnel effect throughout these years is that is creates a terrible disconnect with the agent and the family. Think about this. As an agent, if you open the flood gates and let everyone pour in, how easy will it be to remember each client's name and situations? The odds will not be in your favor. As a kid, you probably attended several birthday parties. How many of you, once the piñata was busted open, stopped to distinctly identify with every piece of candy that you put into your bag? Well, hell no. You ran into the fray and got down and dirty to rake in as much cavity-causing candy as you could, right? The goal was not to identify; it was to collect and discard later. The funnel effect is no different.

Here is the sad thing. Clients have been subjected to this type of practice for so long, they are just used to it. This is not a matter of going to one barber shop for twenty years because they do a great job and know how you like your hair cut. This is a matter of our clients throwing their hand up in the air and saying, "Ah, they're all the same." They know when there is disconnect between them and their insurance agent. They also know when they are just a number in a pool of accounts. The funnel effect can create a bonanza of business for an agent to write and profit from at first. However, insurance doesn't stop at the signing of a deal. The service work will always follow. This is especially true when you do not assess the risks properly and stuff your pipeline with improper accounts.

As a new agent, you should be observant to the fact that funnel agents probably will surpass you in growing their business—at first.

Remember, agents that adhere to the funnel practice almost always are not disciplined enough to handle the rodeo that follows with it. So do not be concerned. Instead, be patient. These agents writing all the funnel business will eventually cohere to the inevitable practice that has given our clients undesirable opinions in the first place. It will happen.

I have made a track-and-field reference already. I will make another. Look at the insurance business this way. Picture the insurance business as the Olympic track. The Olympic track has been used since the eighth-century BC, but the concept has always been the same. It's a footrace around the track and let's see who wins. Funnel agents will take off in a mad fury out of the blocks. You should let them. Eventually, they will run out of gas while you have kept a smart and steady pace the entire time. Sure, they look great at first. Eventually, you will pass them up because you chose the more methodical approach to the race. Writing insurance alongside those funnel agents is no different. It's a marathon, not a sprint. I really believe the hardest thing for an agent to do is to watch these agents explode at first. The competitive nature comes out, and impatience manifests itself. I completely understand how that works, and now I am asking you to understand it as well.

Slow your business down, and pay special attention to detail. It is okay to be particular about the business you write. This will allow you to give your clients more attention and gain more time in getting to know them on a more personal level. Our clients do not want to be a part of an agency who stamps a number on them as they are leaving. They want to know that they matter to their agent. Funnel agents do not realize this analogy. It is a foreign concept to them.

I like to look at funnel business as a glass with a small hole at the bottom. You can pour water in it as often as possible, but the hole will keep it at a constant level for the most part and never really fills up. Condition yourself to understand that this type of practice does exists in your market. Rather than focus on the initial explosion of growth, focus on maintaining a consistent practice that will continue to grow without losing business through the back door. It will be challenging. Your patience will be tested, and you will question as to if your practice is the right way to grow your business. Be confident, and trust your instincts. Once you have recognized how the practices around you are hurting the competition, then you can actually move to providing solutions for everything that is wrong with the funnel effect.

Look at your risk management on a daily basis, and place a very strong emphasis on putting good business on the books. It will take a level of discipline that can be challenging. As long as you convey to your clients that they matter and do everything you can to show them, you will begin to see customer loyalty and retention. More importantly, you will put actions into motion that will change the culture of the insurance business and cast a positive light on the way that it is perceived.

As you are being selective about your business and not subscribing to the funnel effect, you will find it a lot easier to give your clients the attention they deserve. You can educate them on the specifics of their policies that way they can know what to expect in the event of a claim. More importantly, they will begin to take notice to the fact that you are willing to take the time to pay special attention to their needs. Folks, this type of service will resonate with your clients, and the funnel effect will take a back seat to the new culture that you have created. The best part of deciding not to succumb to the funnel effect is that your clients will begin to talk about the different and refreshing encounters they have had with you. There is nothing better for your young career than the power of positive word of mouth.

CHAPTER FIVE

Gatekeepers

There are some insurance agents out there that have been in business for years and years. They have weathered the storms and have grown their business. One thing that I believe to be very important to be aware of is that (sometimes) these tenured agents can become lax. They have plateaued over the years and are very much okay with coasting. There is nothing wrong with this, if you're into that type of thing. You will begin to see that some of these "successful" and tenured agents will have an office full of service reps, producers, and secretaries that will handle a large percentage of their business for them.

Is this a bad thing? Isn't the goal of every insurance agent to grow their business so much that they have to begin hiring staff in order to cover specific service work? It isn't necessarily bad at all. It is a respectable goal to have. I am all for it. Here is where you and I need to be real clear about something. Having administrative staff to help you conduct quality service is not the same as pawning every issue off on someone else in your office to take care of. Here is another trend to be privy on. When clients have an issue, they want to talk to their agent. They don't want to talk to a part-time college student who is there only to answer phones. I do not take away from the fact that good secretaries serve a quality purpose. They do. However, the trend that I have seen is an agent that will take advantage of their administrative staff and force them to handle every issue that arises so they can make their 8:00 a.m. tee time. This is not what the client wants and feeds into their preconceived notions about the insurance industry consisting of wolves only out for themselves.

An agent must be involved with issues that arise from the client. That is the level of service that they deserve. I would never suggest that bringing on staff to aide with customer service is not the right thing to do. That would be crazy. Agents can get spoiled, however. Bringing in a quality service rep that can literally do it all can really put the agent on easy street. We are only human, right? Imagine having a business where you can sit in your office and watch your staff handle everything for you. You can leave whenever you'd like, go play golf, take vacations, etc. I am talking about the good life, the American dream.

I have seen insurance agencies where the agent was literally never around. The agent's name was on the building and on all the billboards but was never there. The agent has an office full of service reps taking care of their clients on issues that should, technically, be handled by the agent. I think over the years that this behavior, even though extremely convenient for the agent, has really sprouted a disconnected consensus between the client and the insurance agent. I really do feel that clients really do want to connect with their agent in a more intimate way. The business of insurance is an intimate business. You are insuring people's most valuable assets, which does require a level of trust and dependency from the client.

Please understand that, as your business grows, adding a workforce to help you with customer service is a definite asset. However you, as the agent, must know not to take advantage of this situation and pile the work load on all your staff. This is especially true when it comes to complicated claims issues, coverage questions, and deep interpretation of the client's insurance policies.

I have always had this specific aggravation when going to the doctor. Thankfully, I haven't had to go to the doctor much throughout my life other than a few minor inconveniences and orthopedic issues. My aggravation would begin the minute I was told that the doctor was busy and could not see me. Instead, they would send medical assistants or nurses to diagnose my problem. I certainly understand that medical assistants and nurses are very knowledgeable in this field and are very valuable in the medical arena. It's not them; it's me. I have always much rather talked to a doctor and hear the news for them. I cannot tell you why, other than it is just a matter of personal preference. It takes away the uneasiness and gives me peace of mind.

I remember flipping through the channels one day and ended up watching a show about tattooing. I have never really thought about the tattoo industry at all. However, I started watching these artists and could not believe how talented they were. Some of the tattoos that these artists were able create on human skin were amazing. The realism, the color saturation, the line work, the list went on and on. True talent was definitely evident. They would interview some of these artists throughout the show so they could share their stories. I remember one of them shared a story about some of his first experiences actually getting tattooed. He found an artist he really liked. He was expensive, but well worth it. He went and visited him a few times for some various tattoos and really got attached to him. Eventually, the artist developed a really good reputation in the community, and his business exploded. Before long, he began hiring other artists and apprentices. His business got so big and lucrative he spent less and less time at the shop. The gentleman they were interviewing went on to say that the next couple of times he went, he actually had to settle for another artist because he was no longer scheduling regular appointments. He wasn't really adamant about seeking his go-to guy going forward. He said, "Looking back, I should've been a little more persistent and demanded my original artist when I went to the shop. Had that been the case, I wouldn't be stuck with these tattoos that looked like they were done by an eight-year-old. I knew they could do okay work, but it wasn't the same as my guy. I was always uneasy just settling, but I wanted to support his new shop with my business."

With this example, I think there is something to be said about the level of comfort that comes with dealing with someone you trust and believe in. When you go and conduct business that is important to you, you do not want to deal with a long line of appointed gatekeepers. You want to deal with the one that is going to give you the best peace of mind.

As a business grows, the need for more personnel grows with it. It just comes with the territory. In the insurance business, not only does an agency grow, but it branches out into different lines of business each needing different levels of attention. For example, a multiline agent can expand their business in lines that expand from auto insurance to major medical insurance. The point to be made is that all lines of insurance have different guidelines, departments, underwriters, and exclusions. It can be a lot for a single agent to tackle. This is where hiring personnel is really advantageous. Here again, once a team is fully cultivated, it is easy for an agent to pass the buck and let them handle just about everything.

Just as insurance has a ton of bells and whistles for an agent to learn, it is even more complicated for a client who knows nothing about it. This is why the client has more peace of mind consulting with their agent and not a gatekeeper. But it happens all the time. This is what your competition could be practicing on a daily basis. What needs to be realized is that the insurance business is not a business in which the agent can be absent on a consistent basis. It is much too important to try and leave on autopilot. We deal with insuring millions of dollars in assets on a daily basis. Not only this, we deal in insuring a family's financial security in case of an untimely death. This list goes on and on. You will run into competitors that simply do not care. They have done their time and are ready to rake in the money and pay little attention to the needs of their clients.

Be there for your clients in their time of need. Reassurance is what they need from their insurance agent. It goes without saying that when someone buys life insurance, they want peace of mind in knowing that their insurance agent will be the one to handle a death claim from beginning to end and not a service rep who is still in the beginning stages of their training.

Hire your staff to help support you in quality service. There is service in the insurance business that service reps can handle just fine. Simple amendments to policies, address changes, trading of vehicles, and faxing paperwork to lenders are all examples of things that they can handle without a problem. However, always be aware of what is going on in your business no matter how minor the issue is. Overseeing the minor issues will definitely let the client know that you are not just all about scoring the big deals and making money off them.

A prospective client actually told me, while I was generating an auto insurance quote, that her old agent would only grace her with his presence when new business was on the table. In other words, he would show little interest in servicing her account until the prospect of writing additional insurance became a reality. That meant more money. You see, clients aren't stupid. They can vividly see when an agent becomes more intrigued with them only when the idea of making more money arises. Once again, these are the types of practices that will give our clients negative opinions about insurance agents and the business in its totality.

When it comes to the competition, I really believe that bad habits develop because agents want to continuously one-up one another. This could not be truer when it comes to gatekeepers and staff. Here is what I mean. The next time you are at a function where there are multiple insurance agents present, go out of your way to engage and listen to what you are hearing. Here is the deal. Insurance agents work diligently to get their businesses off the ground. Many hours and hard work are dispersed on a daily basis in order to get established in their respected markets. There is a tendency, once they are established, to start comparing themselves to what and how their peers are doing.

Before long, there is a stigma. Reputations are now on the line. One agent will take a look at their competition's success and feel like, in order to be successful themselves, they need to cohere with what the others have done and are doing. Before long, there is a sense of "mine is better than yours" and the bragging rights begin. Over the years, I have made the conclusion that the one thing that agents would brag about the most was having a team who literally did everything for them. "I tell you, in my office, I literally do not have to come in every day because my people handle it all," I would hear them say. They believe this is a sign of power, of success. Not only is the agent making money, but they do not even have to come into office to make it.

Do not get caught up in this web. It is this kind of mentality that creates disconnect between the client and the agent in the first place. An agent, with this mentality, has forgotten why they got into this business in the first place. Putting clients first is an afterthought. The integrity of the business has taken yet another sharp blow to the gut and your job to change the culture has just gotten harder. But you can handle it!

CHAPTER SIX

Big Spenders

I have heard before from aspiring agents they feel a bit of an intimidation factor coming into the business. It is important to analyze this and understand why this is the consensus. Depending on your demographic location, your market could be heavily saturated with competition. There may be an insurance agency on every corner. It is easy for an aspiring agent to be a little intimidated driving through town and seeing billboards and other advertising elements all over town. You need to expect that. However, what does this tell you?

To answer that question, most people will say, "Well, that tells me that this insurance agent has been around for a while and has a ton of money to get his/her name out there." Or perhaps, "Well, how in the hell am I going to compete with them? I've only been in this for a month!" You should take a step back and consider what I have come to realize about these "big spenders." Advertising is only half of the battle with trying to gain someone's business. Anyone can drop thousands of dollars a year for advertising. Advertising works. It always has. But it is what you do after all those advertising dollars are spent that matters the most.

You see, I look at advertising differently. Let's say I spend big money on a television commercial for my agency. It is a catchy commercial and has a great time slot every day. Of course this will spark interest and the phone will start to ring. While advertising is used to get the clientele in the door, it is the follow-through and personal connections that are going to keep them on the books. If you do not utilize advertising the right way, all it is going to do is put more water in the perpetual stream and continue building the base of clients that still think we are just a pack of wolves. How, you ask? Well, we have already agreed that the client's perception is there and how it came about. We also know that this industry has fallen victim to countless years of counterfeit service and lack of follow-through. The answer is simple: lack of nurture. You cannot expect to spend thousands of dollars advertising and then do nothing to change the stagnant culture once they come into your office. The client comes in, and you allow your service reps to do all the dirty work and have no desire to meet the client and get to know them. You've hired someone to do all that, right? What has changed?

We have all heard, "You have to spend money to make money." Hey, I agree! Getting your name out there, and being noticed is a huge part of the process. Without going the extra mile and conforming to the consensus, all you will be doing is just the spending part. What are the positives from that? Perhaps it is the write-off aspect, right?

Do not be intimidated because it is reality and will be all around you. Instead take it at face value. There is that term—*face value*. It is what it is. This can work to your advantage. I do not know how many times someone came into my office and had no idea who their previous agent was. They never met them. Can you believe that? I am talking brand insurance companies too. You know, the ones you see on television and such. How can you be an insurance agent for a brand company that we all know and never reach out to your clients to introduce yourself and form a relationship with them? I promise you, it happens all the time. This is not what the client wants. It is more bullshit that has been created by irresponsible agents throughout the years that allows our clientele to depict us as the wolves of insurance.

There is no sense in being disgruntled about it. Remember, it is what it is. However, you can come to terms with the fact that it is reality, and you can start making steps to change the culture. This takes time. One client at a time, you can start to change how others feel about the industry that you love.

I believe that sometimes big spending is just something that agents want to brag about aside from having the big fancy team that does everything for them. At any rate, this issue is still there. Big spending, if there is no follow-through, is just another way to pacify the public into thinking the agent actually cares more than they do. Your competitor may have the billboards, the wrapped vehicle, and the restaurant menu ads, but are they willing to terminate the spending to invest quality time getting to know their clientele? Probably not.

Take the time to get involved with your community functions. There are chamber of commerce events, town festivals, sporting events, etc. In my community, there is a balloon fest that comes to town annually. During this festival, hot-air balloons blanket the fields and bring in the entire town for a weekend of festivities. I have always noticed the big spenders during these events. They make a big presence during the events and put together a lot flare for attention. Be aware though. It isn't enough for the competition to spend big money on these gatherings. They may have the flare and the barbecue pits, but do they have the desire to authentically get to know the people in their community? Or is it more about the bragging rights to the other agents at the bar later that night?

Please understand that the job isn't done when the money is spent. For example, let's say that the biggest charity golf tournament of the year is this weekend. The charity is for pediatric cancer research, and your competition is the biggest sponsor. It is a noble notion that an organization will come out to support such an important cause. So you head to the golf course and immediately begin to notice that the agent that is sponsoring the event is not there. Instead, his office staff is there handing out bottled water, marketing goodies, and business cards. Where's the agent? Nobody's home.

You see, the public needs to see some substance here. They need to see that the insurance agent is there to support the cause above all. Whether it is a charity to help fund cancer research or an annual chamber of commerce mixer, the insurance agent should make a positive impact and truly have a vested interest in supporting the cause at hand. Otherwise, money was spent for no reason other than a tax write-off. Insurance agents are looking to spend money as the answer for all their problems in their market. I have said it a million times during my career, "You cannot buy loyalty." Many agents may think that throwing money around town is somehow going to help them make connections with the clientele. The only thing that throwing money around is going to do is create entitlement issues for the agent. I spent the most money, so therefore, I should be entitled to a larger share of the market. Wrong again.

Advertising is meant to help you get noticed. It is meant to help get people to reach out to you for your services. It isn't meant to somehow mark one's territory in the marketplace. It is a farce to think that someone can automatically lay claim to a specific market just by spending large amounts of money on billboards and such. This is what happens though. There are times when the competition will literally think that they have territories in your community just because of the advertising they have done there. Your market is free for you to grow your business at all times. No one can take that away from you except you.

You will be amazed at the egos you will run into with the big spenders. Be prepared for it, and do not let it phase you in the least. As I mentioned before, it is not enough to spend big money painting the town with your brand. There is way more to it.

One thing that I have noticed over the years with the big spenders is that they rarely come out of their comfort zone. Even though new agents may think that they have the market on lockdown, they don't. It is quite the opposite. How can this be? Well, most insurance agents that I have noticed that spend the money tend to do the same events year after year. Typically, they are the most costly ones. What you need to understand about this is that when you do not think outside the box with your advertising, you are limiting yourself to a certain client base. What you also need to understand about this is that most insurance agents are okay with it. I do not think that spending the big bucks on the big annual events is a bad thing at all. But why stop there? What message are you sending to the public?

You are telling them that you are only interested in swinging for the fences or catching the bigger fish. What about everything in between?

Train yourself to really broaden your areas of interest with advertising. Chances are, you will not be able to be a big spender of advertising right away. That is very much okay. Start with sponsoring Little League teams or local schools in some way. Work with the children in your community to let your clientele know you are ready to make a heartfelt impact. Believe it or not, the outreach with this approach can spread faster throughout town because you are not narrowing your efforts with certain high-end events. Here again, if you keep it simple, it will give you more of an opportunity to connect with your clientele and really focus on what is important to them not you.

I love examining the competition for a multitude of reasons. You can pick up on their habits and really use that to help you grow your own business. In regard to the big spenders, do not conform to the idea that you have to spend a ton of money in order to succeed. You do not have to keep up with the trends in order to grow your business. Remember that the competition has fallen into the same old practices that tend to make the client standoffish no matter how fancy they get with their spending. While the competitors in your area are too busy comparing themselves to one another and trying to continuously one up one another, you can make it a point to change the culture of the business. I believe that the competition will not take the time from writing the big advertising checks to sincerely look for other (less extreme) avenues to make an impact in. I am not saying you cannot spend the big bucks with advertising ever. There is nothing wrong with base hits instead of home runs. If you decide to sign up for the home run derby, do it for the right reasons and do not forget where you came from.

One thing that you should understand about the big spenders is that they feel like they can spend large amounts of money on advertising in lieu of connecting with their clients on a more intimate level. Once again, it does not work that way. Here again, you cannot buy loyalty, and you shouldn't use advertising as a way to conceal the fact that you refuse to get back to your roots and touch lives. Like I said before, spending money on advertising is a way to spark interest and get the phone ringing. It is your responsibility to use the steady flow of client traffic (from advertising and spending money) to perfect your skills on making an impact in your client's lives. Money does not do that on its own—you do. Remember, the competition can be your biggest referral source, especially when they are not impactful and putting themselves before the client.

CHAPTER EIGHT

The Virtual Agent

The crazy thing about being a virtual agent is that some agents are okay with it. Do you remember playing Nintendo when you were young? Do you remember playing those video games that required you to pass levels in order to get to the big boss? It reminds me of what clients have to go through in one of these agencies in order to get to their agent. They have to go through the gauntlet in order to get to the big boss. A lot of the big spenders have put administrative people in place to run interference for them while they rake in the big bucks and hit the country club daily.

There are a variety of insurance companies that offer their services strictly online. Their licensed agents are mostly centrally located and field phone calls from the client when an issue arises. The thing that you must remember about an online service is that the client that chooses this form of service is well aware that the agent only exists over the phone or online. Most of these online companies are very convenient for the client. For the most part, you can submit all your information, and they can quote your business in a very timely manner. This thrifty type of service seems to be able to suit the more active and busier clientele. These companies are meant to exist online exclusively. The idea of the virtual agent is already expected by the client.

Let the online companies secure the virtual agent market. This market is there for a certain type of clientele. What you need to be prepared for with your competition is that they can be perceived as a virtual agent themselves because of the type of practice they have implemented. We discussed earlier that some agents grow so quickly that they hire an assembly line of service reps in order to help them with their daily process. This is where they turn right when they should turn left.

You see, clients that elect to do business with you are not looking for a virtual agent. You will come to see that the art of doing business face-to-face, with a handshake, is still very much what the client is looking for today. Call it the old-school mentality, if you will. I believe that dealing with someone in person is the approach that needs to be taken to earn trust. Your competition may be blind to the fact.

We have discussed preconceived notions quite a bit and how they came about. An insurance agent that is constantly absent will take on the role of the virtual agent and not even know it. They assume that having an office full of service staff will somehow make constant absence justifiable. That isn't how it works. Do not get pulled into this mentality because, eventually, it will be detrimental to your business. In my career, other than price increases, the number one complaint that I received on my competition was the fact that they were never in the office.

Ladies and gentlemen, you have to understand how extremely important our business is. We are literally the ones that will show up to someone's doorstep with a check for indemnification when something catastrophic happens. This could be damage to their home after a fire, a totaled-out vehicle after a crash, or an untimely death that has left a family in peril. When everyone else is asking for money from our clients, we are there to give money so that they can restore their lives after the chaos. What other business does this? When a client needs us the most, we need to be there for them. Some of our competition have forgotten this.

In my opinion, this is one element in a stagnant culture that is the easiest to change. There is no better way for an insurance agent to lose credibility than to be absent at a time of need. People tend to really panic at claim time, especially if it is their first time. They are uneasy, nervous, and uncertain about the process altogether. Depending on the severity of the claim, you could encounter several levels of panic from the client. Obviously, a death claim would warrant a more passionate client than a hail claim to their automobile. Being accessible for your clients is what they will be looking for. If this was not the case, they would've already signed up online to secure a virtual agent.

I mentioned earlier agents that experience rapid growth tend to hire administrative staff to assist them with various aspects of their business. A lot of the time, these service reps get really well versed in the business and do a really great job taking care of the clients. I have seen in the past customer service reps doing such a good job that they refuse to deal with anyone else. This isn't necessarily a bad thing at all. In fact, when a customer service rep is hired, it is the goal of the agent to cultivate them into quality employees.

The idea that some clients become so accustomed to the service reps that they refuse to talk to anyone else may seem like a victory for the agent that has worked so hard to make this a reality. Here is what the competition isn't realizing. There are aspects of the insurance business that can, and should, only be handled by the agent. It seems now that having clients that only feel comfortable speaking to the service reps can be a bit of a handicap.

Let's say that a claims situation arises that can only be handled by the agent. Let's also say that the agent has already cemented a reputation as a virtual agent. The client will automatically feel a little uneasy because they will now have to deal with the virtual agent instead of their go-to service rep. On top of this, the virtual agent isn't accustomed to dealing with the clients anyway. This will lead to a healthy dose of awkward interactions between the agent and the client. Sure, the job may get done. However, this gives the client the opinion that their agent is being very selective about the issues they feel are important enough to tackle.

Being a virtual agent definitely fuels the preconceived notion fire that our clients have about insurance agents. For the most part, I believe that agents find success in being able to leave the office in the hands of their service reps on a consistent basis. It's the American dream, remember? It doesn't take long for the clients to take notice of the virtual agent. I ask that you recognize that virtual agents do exist in your market. As these agencies begin to grow, it is very common for the agent to become scarce in the office.

As an agent of change, please recognize these trends with the competition in your area. These agents place their agencies on auto-pilot and tend to rely on their administrative staff to run the day-to-day operation. The client wants to be able to talk to their agent when there is an issue. Remember, they are not the expert in the insurance business. They will prefer to talk to someone, in person, about their claim and not have to go through an assortment of telephone reps to find the answer. Make it a point to be there for your clients no matter how minor the issue is. Leave the virtual agents for the competition. Either way, you will not be a part of the general consensus that portrays insurance agents as wolves in suits.

You

CHAPTER NINE

The Observer

We have spent a lot of time talking about what to expect from your clients and the competition. I feel it is very important to go a little deeper in discussion about the most important element in the insurance business: you. We can go on and on about what to expect from the outside world as you immerse yourself in the insurance business, but it's really how you condition your mind and heart that is going to pinpoint the direction that you and your business go.

The insurance business isn't for everyone. It takes a level of dedication from the agent in order to carry out the duties of insuring what is near and dear to someone's heart. You have to really open your mind and heart to the people you serve in order to grasp the importance of providing security for them and the ones they love. I mentioned before that keeping your head on a swivel was the way to go—I meant it.

What you will come to see early in your insurance career is that everyone is different. No two people that you will deal with are exactly alike. Some people are more passionate and others aren't. As an agent, I feel it is absolutely crucial to train yourself to be the best observer as possible. I mentioned earlier that being a great listener is imperative. After all, in order to be a great observer, you have to be a great listener.

You will come to find out that some clients are more meticulous about things than others. This must be embraced. For example, let's say that you have someone that wants to put their auto policy premiums on bank draft because the thought of paying $1.50 installment fee brings about thoughts of an impending apocalypse. I joke when I say that, but there are people that you will encounter that absolutely refuse to shell out an additional $1.50 if they don't have to. There are clients out there who couldn't care less. They mail off a monthly check or process an online credit card payment and get hit with the installment fee, and they move on with their lives not giving a second thought about it. As an agent, you cannot assume that everyone will be all right with paying the $1.50. If you get in this frame of mind and encounter someone who is set off by paying the fee, your client will be extremely upset that you have made your assumption. Thus, this will give the client the notion that every insurance company out there wants to bleed the customer for every dime they can. It may sound a little dramatic, but I promise you, you will encounter this situation more than a few times.

We have discussed how some clients, because of elements out of your control, will be extremely guarded when they step into your office. Here again, they are guarded because of years and years of the same thing without fail. Train yourself to notice this when they come in. Some of the signs will be a reluctance to give you information, lack of eye contact, disengagement, and a tendency to be in a rush. One word for how you can slowly turn this ship around comes to mind: *consistency*. You see, your clients will act this way because of what they are expecting from another regular insurance agent. They feel like nothing is going to change. You must observe these signs because they will very quickly be thinking, *What makes this agent so different from the others?*

If you are consistent in giving your clientele the attention they deserve, then they might have a change of heart sooner than you think. Your clients should be engaged with you at all times. If you show them that you are actually interested in something other than taking their money, then they may look at you a little differently. People have a tendency to be scared of what they do not understand. This couldn't be more true than in the insurance industry. You have to make it make sense for them. If you are consistently taking time to get to know them on a more personal level, then you have already begun to break the mold of being a wolf of insurance.

Once you have identified the signs of disengagement, then it is easy to provide the client with a solution for the things that have tainted their perception of the insurance agent to begin with. There may be clients out there with very complicated lines of business. Perhaps they have personal lines of business, commercial, or farm and ranch. These clients tend to always be uneasy because they know that their situations are atypical to insure. Aside from this, these clients tend to have a preconceived notion that their agent will not spend the time to review their policies correctly because of the complexity of their situations. They're right. I have seen agents throughout the years balk at the opportunity to sit down with these clients and go over their insurance policies with a fine-tooth comb. It must be done! If you take the time to review the client's policies, this will show them that they do matter to you, and you are willing to take time out of your schedule to make sure they are adequately covered.

I am a big believer in karma. It is one of the few things in life that actually terrifies me. It seems that karma is *always* present in the insurance business. Being an observer, you can always have a head start in identifying those that are yearning for someone to give them a little more attention. Give them the attention they want and deserve! For those agents that simply do not make time to review their clients, they are opening themselves up to more problems and altercations than they realize. Policies that are not regularly reviewed, at the client's request, are more subject to errors and omission situations than others. If you do not take the time to adhere to your client's requests, karma will come back during claim time, I can promise you that.

Being observant of your clients is so important in determining the type of service they require. Remember, no two people are identical. As an insurance agent, one of the most difficult parts of your job will be to decipher the various types of personalities that you will encounter on a daily basis. You wear many hats as an agent. One minute you could be dealing with someone who is overly emotional after a claim, and the next minute you will be dealing with someone who is adamant about going over the fine print in their life insurance policy.

I am reminded of a story that a colleague told me early in my career. We all know that a beneficiary has to be named when someone purchases a life insurance policy. Whether it is a spouse, sibling, child, or a grandchild, the beneficiary is the one that is chosen by the insured to handle the proceeds after a claim is paid out due to death. People tend to buy life insurance because they love someone. A beneficiary is someone the insured not only trusts but loves as well. It is a high honor, if you ask me. This colleague had written a life insurance policy on an acquaintance and her husband at the time. I remember he was always talking about how high maintenance this lady was. She had a ton of questions about the policy before, during, and after the policy was written. He readily admitted that, after the policy was a done deal, he was ready to have it behind him. I remember him saying, "It's a good thing life insurance doesn't require a lot of service work after the sale because I don't know how much more of that woman I could handle."

This agent always had a way of not really conforming to each different client that walked into his office. He had the exact process for every customer that he dealt with. Not good at all. The lady called the agent about a year later. I remember the secretary buzzed him in his office and said, "It's the lady you can't stand!" I remember hearing the moaning and groaning coming out of his office once he was told who it was. Evidently, the woman had a very nasty divorce from her husband, whom she had three children with in their ten years together. I cannot tell you what exactly happened to cause the messy divorce. What I can tell you is that she called the agent and demanded that he removed her husband as beneficiary from the life policy and replace him with her sister.

Due to the fact that the agent could not stand this woman because of how high maintenance she was, he told her that he would mail a change form to her so that she could fill it out and mail it back to him. The agent elected this method because he refused to have her come in and field the ton of questions that she would probably have about the simple process. The agent could not conform to the various types of personalities he would be dealing with, so he subsequently excommunicated this woman because he only knew of one way to deal with every client in his book of business and she did not fit his standard of comfort. There was no adaptation to her different style of demand.

The agent mailed off the form and received it a few days later. In the return envelope was the amended form that listed the woman's sister as beneficiary. Along with this form was a short letter that the woman had written to the agent. In a nutshell, the letter to the agent expressed how important it was to the woman that this change be done proficiently and quickly. It also went on to actually mention some of the specifics about why the divorce came to fruition. From what I recall, the husband was not a very nice man at all, and there were safety concerns that the woman had for her and the children.

The agent, over the years, could not get used to dealing with clients that did not fit his style of business. Instead of being observant and adapting to the various types of personalities and preferences each client displayed, he made them conform to him and his preferred style of business. The agent ended up putting the amended beneficiary change form on the back burner. The woman was so adamant about removing the ex-husband as beneficiary, she went on to state in the letter that she did not believe he would secure their children's future with the funds. She believed he would take the money to fulfill his own agenda.

Four months later, the woman is killed by a drunk driver. She was thirty-one years old. You guessed it. The agent had not followed through with the change, and the ex-husband received a quarter of a million dollars in tax-free death proceeds. The children never saw a penny of that money. The sister of the dearly departed ended up visiting the agent a few weeks later. She was distraught and pleaded with the agent to do something to help out the situation. There was nothing that could be done. What a terrible situation for the woman's surviving children.

The agent needed to understand beforehand that dealing with different people warrants an adaptation on his end. You *cannot* expect your clients to inconvenience themselves by having to conform to your one-dimensional style of customer service. It is a selfish practice and does not support the idea of putting all clients ahead of yourself. All this agent needed to do was to realize that this woman required a little more attention and follow suit. Had he done this, a simple transaction would've been completed, and he would've been delivering the woman's sister a check to help support the surviving children that had been abandoned by their father. Instead, he deemed dealing with this woman as an inconvenience to him, and now her children have to suffer for his lack of adaptation.

That story is a painful way to learn a very valuable lesson in insurance. Once you step into this business, you have to understand that different people are going to require different levels of attention. Knowing this will be advantageous in that you can begin to train yourself to notice how people react to you and what they are expecting from you. Giving the clients something new to look at will only heighten their ability to trust you and give you a fighting chance. Be open to the different personalities that you will encounter and be empathetic to your clients no matter what. You do not know what they have been through or what they are going through. People process adversity differently. Some clients may struggle dealing with peril, and others can handle it. Your mistake is assuming that everyone can handle it. They may need your help.

On the other side of the spectrum, eventually you will become an expert in identifying with the many types of personalities you will be dealing with. Oddly enough, you will have fun with it! How boring would it be if everyone that walked into your office was exactly the same? Take it as a challenge. Learn about your clients and understand them on a more personal level. Learn their habits, know what they expect, and conform to them in order to carry out their needs. When you do this, your clients are no longer numbers on the wall. They are people that matter to you, and you are willing to give them the attention they are yearning for, and you do this by simply observing.

CHAPTER TEN

Financial Reality

I have always rejected the term salesman. To me, the term *salesman* has always implied someone who just takes and never gives. Perhaps I have fallen into a preconceived notion myself. The reality is, insurance is in the sales arena. That is what the insurance business is.

There are many people throughout time that have made a great living at sales. Whether it is selling jewelry, cars, or insurance, it does take a certain type of person to be able to connect with the public. Many businesses offer an hourly wage or an annual salary to their employees. An hourly wage or an annual salary constitutes a level of comfort (or safety net) that many accept as a viable way to make a living and support their families.

When you hear the word sales, one word comes to mind: *commission*. Commission is a certain percentage that is paid to the producer as it pertains to the amount of money they moved the product for. Let me give you an example. Let's say a realtor sells a house for $300,000. The percentage of commission for their services is 3 percent of the sales, so the realtor will collect $9,000. Obviously, there are some realtors that make an exceptional living selling houses. They continue to pound the pavement and search for inventory to get a listing on.

Insurance is the same way. An insurance agent collects a percentage of commission for the sale of an insurance policy just like any other sales position. However, this is where the insurance business differs from your traditional "commission for just what you sell" type business. Let me tell you what I mean about that. While there are certain sales businesses that offer a small base plus commission, most sales positions offer commission based on only what you sell. Real estate is a great example. Real estate agents are some of the hardest working people in the world. The competition is fierce, especially when inventory is low. Once they collect on a sale, they move onto the next listing. Insurance agents do make a commission on the insurance policies they sell. The percentages differ according to what type of policy you write. However, an insurance agent's portfolio is usually vast and offers a large array of products to offer the public according to the need. It literally makes you more versatile in the avenues you can take to serve the public.

Aside from the variety of different portfolio options an insurance agent has, there is one very important fundamental advantage the insurance business has over the rest. It's called residuals. Remember that word, residuals. One more time, residuals.

Here is what I *love* about how the insurance business typically compensates an insurance agent. Let's say you write a six-month automobile insurance policy for someone. At the inception of the policy, you will be compensated a certain percentage for the six month total premium. For example, 10 percent (commission on six-month premium) of $1,000 (six-month total policy premium) is $100. Here is where you need to get excited. The majority of insurance companies out there will pay you a residual commission when the policy you write renews. Most of the time, the residual commission is a little smaller than the original commission paid; sometimes it is not. Let's take the 10 percent example I just gave you. When that auto insurance policy renews in six months, you get paid again! So in this case, let's say it is 7 percent. So at renewal, you will get paid on that policy $70. Residual income is a huge part of the insurance business, and this is where our industry stands out in my opinion.

Now that we have discussed the semantics on how insurance commissions work, let's talk about why residuals is so important and why this ties into everything you have read in this book so far. When you consider a career in insurance, have longevity in your mind and heart. Residual income does you no good if you take tenure off the table. Remember when I said that insurance was a marathon not a sprint? That analogy applies to so much in this business.

The goal, as an insurance agent, is to continue to grow your base year after year. You want to continue to have the meter running at all times. All the business your write will eventually be up for renewal. If you are doing your due diligence, the business will stay on the books and renew as scheduled. So in essence, you started with a snowball, and your goal is to make it bigger and bigger as time goes by.

If a policy is up for renewal and the client does not renew, you simply will not be compensated for it, and you have lost a piece of your snowball. There are times that a client may cancel a policy mid-term. This could be because they found a different carrier, moved out of state, or have passed away. If there is unearned premium from that policy period, you may be charged back a percentage for that commission. Unearned premium will never be the full amount you were originally compensated, so do not be worried. However, it is important to know that this may occur.

Remember, the meter is running. I like to look at residual income a certain way. As time goes by, you will build your snowball. I have always said that if an insurance agent can keep a steady flow of new business over time, they will start getting compensated at midnight every night while they sleep. You can literally make money while you sleep if you choose to look at it that way! Every night at midnight, a new day starts, and a policy will renew. That residual commission will be there waiting for you.

I like to compare the insurance commission structure to a traditional savings account at a bank. Let's think about that. With a traditional savings account, a person will take money out of their income flow and deposit it to the savings. Obviously, as time goes by, the amount grows as deposits are made. There will be times when money will be taken out from time to time as circumstances arise. The goal here again is to continue to make deposits and grow the account as much as possible and minimize extractions. What does it take to grow your account? It takes discipline. Making sure your policies stick and renew takes discipline, and that is the ultimate challenge for the insurance agent.

We have spent a lot of a lot of time talking about what to expect from the existing cultures of the insurance business. I believe compensation is an important part of it because it is a different animal. Maintaining a healthy income in the insurance business is challenging but extremely attainable. However, you do have to know how it works. Knowing the mechanics of how it works will definitely prepare you for what you will have to do (mentally) to successfully grow.

You know that writing business is not enough. You must write the business and maintain it for future growth. In order to do this, you will have to keep learning how to observe your clientele. Bring it all together. Use what you have learned so far to find solutions for the preconceived notions that have crippled the insurance industry. Only then will you be able to keep clients, earn your residuals, and continuously grow.

Folks, there is no ceiling on the monetary possibilities that the insurance business may bring you. You are in complete control of your monetary gains, and no one will tell you what you are worth. You have to go out in the market and earn what *you* feel you are worth. Do not be intimidated by commission structures. You are being paid for earning people's trust and protecting what is near and dear to their hearts. Patience is definitely the key. Trust isn't earned overnight. Always remember that commission sales require trust in yourself as well. You have to trust your ability to be a person of positive impact in your market.

CHAPTER ELEVEN

Is It about You?

I sincerely believe that there is a direct correlation between the public's perception about the insurance business and how you must look within your heart before you even begin to write business. In the insurance business, you will offer customer service, various insurance policies, claims service, etc. However, the most important element you can offer your clients is *you*. But is it always going to be about you? If you are thinking yes, then give yourself a pat on the back because you just told yourself exactly the opposite of where this thought process is going. It's okay, however. We are still going to make it make sense.

Early in my career, I worked alongside a very interesting gentleman. We will call him Donald. Donald was the poster boy of what insurance companies were looking for. He was young, energetic, persistent, and never took no for an answer. Now, it is no secret that many insurance companies can offer very nice incentives for producing agents. There is a reason I have not really touched on the incentives that may exists within the insurance business. But we'll get into that later.

Donald was extremely goal-oriented. It did not matter what the incentive was. He was going after it with a level of aggression that could only be rivaled by a wolf. Donald had a major problem, however. In his quest to conquer his goals and win his incentives, he lost focus on what he was there to do. He starting looking at his clients as stepping stones to win his next trip. Personal empathy and consideration were out the window in order for him to hop on that plane and travel on the company's dollar. "I have to find one more sucker to sign on the dotted line so I can win my damn trip!" he would say. "They can run, but they can't hide!" was another one of his favorites.

I remember listening to this man interact with his clients, and it was like hearing a fork on a chalkboard. It was offensive the way he strong-armed the client in order to carry out his own agenda. There was no substance or integrity in the way he was conducting his business. These people came to him in good faith to find coverage for the things that meant the most to them.

Donald kept his practice going for a while. He continued to earn his incentives and bonuses. Eventually, he realized one thing: he wasn't growing. Remember, we spent the last chapter going over how the commission structure with insurance works. He became reliant on day-to-day sales. Sure, he met his goals this way by keeping his nose to the grindstone. However, his residuals were not panning out. The business he wrote was not staying around to see him off at the airport. He was consumed with himself and not taking his client's interests to heart.

Let me tell you why his residuals were not panning out. Donald was so aggressive with his sales tactics, he fell right into the flowing stream that is the preconceived notion. His business became a business of quoting. There was absolutely no substance. The clientele came in, got the quote, committed, and then shopped around at renewal. No residual income was to be earned.

This business is not about you! It's about the lives you impact by truly caring and taking the time to make sure that each family you come into contact with is safely secure. I mentioned before how competitive the insurance business can be. When someone walks into your office, understand that they had dozens of options for an insurance quote. The wrong type of insurance agent will make these people a statistic. The right type of insurance agent will not take them for granted and truly show an interest in them.

An insurance agent has a responsibility to the community as a person of positive influence. A personal connection must be made by the agent and the client at all times. As I mentioned earlier in the book, the client does not want to spend hours out of their day talking about you. As human beings, we want the chance to share with the world all our success stories. Take a look at social media. Social media is chock-full of people that embellish at the opportunity to post pictures of their children, their homes, and everything that they are proud of in their lives. People work hard to provide for their families, and that is why they walk into an insurance agency to begin with—to protect all that they have worked hard for their entire lives. Open yourself up to your clients. Put yourself on the back burner for a moment to hear these success stories. You will be astonished at what you learn about the very people that walk along side of you in your community. You will hear trials and tribulations, victories, struggles, and spiritual growth.

In my career, I have always loved to hear my clients' stories about rising after falling in life. There is something to be said about someone who hits rock bottom then proceeds to pick themselves up and achieve redemption in the form of perseverance. The transformation that one makes on the road to redemption is very inspiring. Wait, what? That's right. It is very possible to be inspired by your clients. If you are willing to let them, they may teach life lessons that you never dreamed of learning otherwise. Perhaps I should say these life lessons would be completely unexpected. I mentioned earlier that an insurance agent needs to be someone who touches lives. If you are willing to open your mind and heart to your clients, *you* can be the one that is touched.

You see, clients aren't expecting to sit across someone at an insurance agency and share the stories that mean the most to them. Perhaps they have never encountered someone who cares about them enough to ask in the least. I always enjoy talking to my elderly clients the most. I made a decision a long time ago to absolutely be willing to hear their stories. They have the best stories. Some of their stories inspired me to no end, especially the ones about long-lasting marriage.

Bob-O used to come into my office a lot to visit with me about everything. Donald would've never made the time. Bob-O was ninety-one years old at the time of his death. He was a veteran and would always tell me stories about all the places in the world he had seen. He said that out of all the countries he had visited in his life, his favorite was New Zealand. Not only was he drawn to the beautiful scenery, but the people as well. New Zealand, back in the late forties, had a mix of New Zealand and Polynesian cultures alike. I remember him saying, "There is a reason why them Polynesians are so big… They eat nine times a day!" He said Polynesian food was the best in the world.

What I admired the most about Bob-O was the fact that he had been married almost seventy years at the time of his death. His wife was a Southern belle from Biloxi, Mississippi, that he met while stationed at Keesler Air Force Base. She was a nurse and an Ol' Miss alumni. Regretfully, I never met Maggie. I wish I would have. Evidently, Miss Maggie had a hell of a right cross according to Bob-O. He experienced it firsthand when he tried to kiss her for the first time. "You're not smooching me until you go to church with me, sir," she informed him. "I spent almost an hour shaving and getting myself all cleaned up that night. I had my fancy service uniform on and the cheapest 'fancy' smell-good cologne I could find. I looked good. She knew I looked good too. She was just playing hard to get. All for her to turn around and sock me a good one on my right eye when I tried to give her an innocent kiss. I had to go back to the base and tell everyone I got clipped kicking someone's ass that was trying to mess with my woman," he confessed.

What a guy. I was willing to open myself up and take a vested interest in his life to hear his stories. They were inspiring, funny, sad, and full of wisdom. One day he came into my office to pay a bill. Normally, my secretary would take his payment, but he would always ask if I was available to hear some of his lies. He came back and we started chatting again. I stared at him for a moment and realized I wasn't paying attention to a single word he was saying, which was rare. My wife and I were newlyweds and were struggling with our communication at the time. She was on my mind, so my attention to Bob-O was a little lackluster that day. He stopped talking and I didn't even realize it.

"You all right, Johnny?" he asked.

I remember it took me a while to answer. Once I regained my focus, I asked him, "Bob-O, I really admire you for too many reasons to count. But the number one reason I admire you is because you have been married to the same woman for almost seven decades. I can't even imagine. Wow. I want to ask you for a favor."

"Lay it on me, son," he tells me.

It took a minute, but I said, "What is your secret, Bob-O? Seventy years, man. I've been married two years, and I'm a little lost. I love my wife more than anything, but sometimes I feel like I take the wrong turn at every corner. What is the best marital advice an expert like you can give me?"

He looked at me with his big eyes that were magnified by his thick lenses. He cracks a smile and says, "Keep your mouth shut!"

I busted out in laughter partly because I thought he was kidding. He remained looking at me as serious as could be. I realized he wasn't kidding.

"Really?" I said.

"You damn straight, son. Keep your mouth shut, and you'll be all right," he said wholeheartedly.

I'll tell you this. That has been the best marital advice I have *ever* received. Bob-O was a straight shooter and one of the greatest men I have ever encountered. He touched my life and made me want to be a better man, father, and husband. I will forever be indebted to him. He lived a long and happy life with his true love, Ms. Maggie. They passed away within nine months of each other. Both died in their sleep. I'll never forget Bob-O.

I could've been the prototypical insurance agent when it came to Bob-O. I could've closed myself off to him, had him sign his contract, collected my commission, and sent him on his way. I'm sure that is what he expected. I'm also sure that is what he had experienced before in the past. Always remember, in the quest to impact a person's life, it is very possible that the person will impact yours as well. But you have to be willing to take a genuine interest in the person sitting across from you. I choose to believe that it can become a symbiotic relationship fairly quickly. Even though your client's have never been in the insurance business before, you can learn things from them that will help you cultivate your business to add integrity and quality. Bob-O taught me that love was the most powerful force on earth. He taught me that being a man of your word builds trust, integrity, and connections. I use his teachings in my business a lot.

You will never learn any life lessons if you omit the opportunity to listen to your client's success stories. The more you hear, the more you will learn. Some of these lessons will be so impactful, you can integrate them into your life and business practice. As I mentioned before, even though the most important thing you can offer your clients is you, the client needs to come first. Taking a genuine interest in them will let them know that you are a different breed of insurance agent. You are someone who cares to learn about the real person inside of them. Slowly, but surely, you will help cast a light on the shadow that has been looming over the insurance business for ages.

If you decide to place your clients first, the benefit you will receive will be far more valuable than the monetary gain. It's a win-win situation. You will be touching lives and being open to having your life touched just the way I did with Bob-O. Most importantly, you are changing the culture of the business and letting the public know that you are here to make an impact and change the consensus. All of a sudden, you no longer run in a pack of wolves. You have separated yourself from the pack—a lone wolf.

CHAPTER TWELVE

Agent of Change

We have been discussing what I feel are some of the most important elements to recognize when pursuing a career in the insurance business. The element of surprise has never been one of my favorite things. In fact, if you were to ask, being blindsided is probably my biggest pet peeve. Preparation and communication are two things that could really prevent getting blindsided, both of which we have discussed.

In the insurance business, you will encounter hundreds of different people who each have their own way of doing business and who have their own perceptions of the insurance business in its entirety. There is nothing you will be able to do about this going in. However, after reading this book, hopefully you can prepare yourself for the consensus and trends that are already typically established before you get there. I only see this as an advantage. Let's leave the blindsiding to the football games. It has no place in the insurance business at all.

As an insurance agent, you must be authentic in business and in life. If you think clients cannot tell when someone is blowing smoke, you are sorely mistaken. They're not stupid. They can also tell when they are being presented a process. The concept of the opening, fact-finding, presentation, and the close (while maybe effective) is not that hard to pinpoint by the client. They will know that they are being presented with some sort of script. The problem with that is there is no substance. There is no personal connection or relationship building. It is a stagnant practice.

There is an old theory in the insurance business called the law of large numbers. It's fairly simple. The more people you come in contact with, the more policies you will write. Sure, coming in contact with people and increasing activity is a part of it, but there is a missing element to that. You have to go that extra mile. Once you have the traffic, take the time to show each and every one of them that you are here to do things differently. Perhaps they will be the ones to get blindsided—in a good way!

Now that you know some of the major trends in the insurance culture, I implore you to be the agent of change that we have been speaking about. You have taken the time to listen to your clients and conform your dealings to what makes *them* feel the securest. You have spent time studying the competition and learning how they have created an unpopular consensus in the insurance community. You have also spent time learning how *you* will change for the better when you finally decide to take that leap of faith into the land of wolves.

If you separate yourself from the wolf pack, as a lone wolf, you will start to see your clientele realize that you are presenting an alternative look at the insurance business. What follows next is the best advertising in the world. You will have ambassadors for your brand that will use their positive words to spread the love about you and the new atmosphere you have brought to the insurance realm. What is even better about that? It doesn't cost you a penny! We talked about the big spenders who would rather spend money to try and buy loyalty rather than create substance and connect intimately with their clients. You cannot buy loyalty in the insurance business, I don't care who you are.

The clients that stay loyal are the ones that you have made a difference in their lives. You have learned about their families and realized the love that exists in their house before you discuss life insurance with them. Or you hear about how proud a father is of his sixteen-year-old daughter for being a model student before you write the auto insurance policy for the new Mustang he just bought her.

Hear the story first. Take in the clients' stories, and maybe you will learn to never take for granted the things that make life worth living. Along the way, I can promise you, you can learn life lessons that will make you better in business and in life itself.

Think about that. Your activity is up and you are experiencing high traffic in your office. You are literally opening the door to hundreds of people that are longing for someone to share their stories with. You will meet inspiring people that you can take lessons from to make your life better. As for the client, they will meet an agent of change and someone who has made up their mind that they will not contribute to the preconceived notions about the insurance industry that have been around for years. You are helping them, and they are helping you. But remember, keep it in order. They come first at all times.

When you decide to become an agent of change and you change someone's negative perception about the insurance agent, it will be more gratifying than writing that huge insurance policy that you've been waiting for. Why is that? Well, you have immersed yourself in an industry that has had a reputation of having wolves as representatives. It is hard to lower your shoulders and push through eighty-mile-an-hour winds. However, when you do, you realize that you have achieved the ultimate goal of changing someone's passionate feelings about an agelong perception. Real change begins with someone's willingness to go against the grain no matter how high the odds are stacked up against them. Once you make up your mind that you will make a difference, the consistency and follow-through will be of the upmost importance. It will not be easy. You may get a taste of satisfactory commissions by succumbing to the funnel effect and may decide to let your foot off the gas for a while and initiate the autopilot.

An agent of change has to look past the temporary successes of the competition. That will definitely be difficult. Seeing all the big names on the billboards and television commercials can definitely be intimidating. That is normal. Keep your concentration on what matters the most: integrity and interest in the client. The agents that take off like a rocket by sinking into self-absorbed practice will rarely last. It is a living day-by-day practice. Residuals will not pan out, and you will have the small hole at the bottom of the glass effect. You can fill it up as aggressively as you may, but it will never surpass a certain level.

As the race continues, those that sprinted are now getting fatigued. You, on the other hand, have a clean, steady pace and are still blowing and going. The insurance business takes time to grow. Time will be on your side if you let it. You will learn how each one of your clients prefer to be taken care of by understanding that every one of them is unique in their own right. Do not waste your time using a one-dimensional approach to conducting your business. It will take time, as well, to become an expert at dealing with different people and personalities. Listen to them. An agent of change understands that a robotic process does not work for everyone. Instead, an agent of change must be a chameleon and adapt to each client. After all, it is not the clients' responsibility to conform to you; it is your responsibility to conform to them.

Lastly, once you have assumed the role of an agent of change, make sure to celebrate your successes. The insurance business, in my opinion, is one of the most rewarding businesses in the world. You are commissioned to help protect the things that mean the most to people. What matters to people may vary because people vary. "Press hard, the bottom copy is yours" is not the way to go. You have to decide if you will join the wolf pack or be the lone wolf that changes the territory for the better. At the end of the day, after you have secured a loving family with a life insurance policy, insured a teenager's first vehicle, or written a policy to insure a dream house that a family has been working their entire lives to save up for, be there for them in the most intimate and authentic way possible. Be sure to reflect on the meaning of how impactful that is because you were one of the ones that made this special moment happen. Take time to celebrate with your family, and do something impactful for them as well. Take that family trip you have been saving for, or buy your spouse that gift they have had their eye on for some time now. What good you do for your clients can be reciprocated to the ones you love as well. They deserve it because they are the greatest support system you will ever have.

Enjoy your successes during your career. Make yourself available to those who need you in the time of peril. After you are confident in understanding what to expect, do everything in your power to change the culture of the insurance industry one client at a time. You can do it! Be authentic, be sincere, and make your clients the most important aspect of your business and you will experience immense growth, both as an agent and person of influence.

From the bottom of my heart, I wish you well in your career, and I hope reading this book has helped you prepare for what lies ahead. Enjoy the rewards, but remember the rewards should be deposited in your heart, not just your bank account. Be an agent of change, and make a difference in the way they perceive the business and the wolves of insurance. Defy the odds. Above all, have fun!

ABOUT THE AUTHOR

 John William Brown Jr. has been in the insurance business for over ten years. Being involved in different lines of businesses throughout his career, he quickly realized that mental conditioning was a vital prerequisite for the insurance industry and aspiring agents. John has been successful in multiline insurance sales and has worked his way into management by enabling himself to adapt to his clients' needs and taking the time to examine the various types of personalities he would be dealing with on a daily basis to provide adequate protection and earn trust. As his business evolved, and management obligations began, John decided to focus on helping other agents (new or tenured) mentally prepare for what the insurance industry would present on a daily basis that most would be unprepared for coming in. John lives in West Texas with his wife, Alisia, of eleven years, and his daughter, Amaya.

CPSIA information can be obtained
at www.ICGtesting.com
Printed in the USA
LVOW12s1032110717
540969LV00001B/120/P